Letters of
Fanny Brawne to Fanny Keats

Fanny Brawne
from the original miniature in the possession
of her grand-daughter Mrs Oswald Ellis

LETTERS OF

FANNY BRAWNE TO FANNY KEATS

1820–1824

Edited with a Biographical Introduction
BY FRED EDGCUMBE

Resident Curator of the Keats Memorial House
Hampstead

WITH A PREFACE

BY MAURICE BUXTON FORMAN

NEW YORK

OXFORD UNIVERSITY PRESS

1937

*Published under the auspices of the Public
Libraries Committee of the Hampstead
Borough Council by whom Keats House
and the Keats Museum are maintained
and administered.*

(LIONEL R. McCOLVIN, F.L.A.
Chief Librarian and Curator)

PREFACE

THE whirligig of time, says the clown in *Twelfth Night*, brings in his revenges. Time in this case has sped a good hundred years, and chance, of which we are told this restless world is full, has brought good fortune in one hand and but a modicum of revenge in the other. And surely chance must have had some guiding finger to point the way for a mere bundle of letters written by one ordinary mortal to another—the sister of one she loved. Ordinary? Yes, for what were these girls if not of the average middle-class type, born and brought up according to their station in life, to be loved, to be married, to bear children, and to pass on unnoticed by the world at large and utterly unknown to later generations had it not been that the one loved a great poet and the other was the poet's sister. Even so it was by mere chance that these letters came home, for the poet's sister once lost many of her belongings while travelling abroad, yet these were saved to her, saved with other letters she held precious, letters counted by us worthy of a shrine in the nation's Valhalla for literary treasures. And now after a long journey by a circuitous route they have come to their final resting place in the demesne whence they issued forth to pass from Hampstead to Walthamstow, from Walthamstow back to Hampstead for a while, then to Spain, and thence, after more than half a century of rest, to start again for Hampstead on that aforesaid roundabout journey, the details of which may not be disclosed. That matters not. There they are and there they will remain, and we may only record our gratitude to time and chance for the gift.

Revenge here has no sinister intent. All it amounts to is that Fanny Brawne emerges from some obscurity to refute silently and with dignity the unkind things that have been said about her in bygone days. No one is hurt. Many will be glad, the many who had faith in her and belief in her love for John Keats, the many who had faith, too, in the poet, who saw through the cloak of the 'minx' and the occasional frequenter of garish assemblies and found beneath it a woman to love, to adore with a passion that spent itself only with his last breath.

These friendly, affectionate, homely letters, edited by Mr. F. Edgcumbe with the care of an enthusiast, may prove sad reading to some, but to those who reach into the truth of things and take pleasure in knowing all that is to be known of those whose lives were intimately in touch with that of Keats, they cannot fail to be of interest. Save for the poet's letters and the few comments made by Gerald Griffin to members of his family, they are the only contemporary and unbiased evidence we have of Fanny Brawne's nature, and they prove her to have been just as I have already said, an ordinary person of sound common sense and good and faithful heart. She was a girl when she first met Keats; she may have been a 'minx'; she became a woman when she said goodbye to him at Hampstead on Wednesday the 13th of September 1820.

M. BUXTON FORMAN

CONTENTS

ILLUSTRATIONS

NOTE

References in the notes are to the following books:

Letters of John Keats.
> Edited by Maurice Buxton Forman, 2nd ed., with revisions and additional letters. 1935. (Letters.)

John Keats, his Life and Poetry, &c.
> By Sir Sidney Colvin. 1917. (Colvin.)

John Keats.
> By Amy Lowell. 2 vols. 1925. (Lowell.)

Life and Letters of Joseph Severn.
> By William Sharp. 1892. (Sharp.)

INTRODUCTION

THE letters here printed, thirty-one in number, were written between September, 1820, and June, 1824. These two dates are significant in the correspondence, as they mark events of striking importance in the lives of both the writer and the recipient. Fanny Brawne said farewell to Keats when, accompanied by Joseph Severn, he left Wentworth Place for Italy and death on September the 13th, 1820; her first letter to his sister is dated September the 17th. Fanny Keats became of age and her own mistress on June the 3rd, 1824, and the final letter of the series is dated a fortnight later.

These letters have had a chequered history. Written at Wentworth Place, Hampstead, from that portion of the building where Keats spent his last days in England, they are addressed either to No. 4 Pancras Lane, Cheapside, the city residence of Mr. Richard Abbey, the guardian of the Keats children, or to Marsh Lane, Walthamstow, Essex, his summer residence, then situated in London's country-side. When Fanny Keats married Señor Llanos y Guiterez in 1826 and subsequently went to Spain she took with her these letters together with those from her brother now in the British Museum and Keats House. As she faithfully observed his wish—'You will preserve all my letters'—they were, at her death, amongst her most treasured possessions. The existence of the letters from Fanny Brawne was undreamt of. The remark by Mrs. Brawne in a letter to Joseph Severn (February 6th, 1821, Sharp's *Life of Severn*, p. 80), 'Fanny and she [Fanny Keats] have constantly corresponded since he left England,' gave no direct clue to the existence of such important biographical documents either to Sir Sidney Colvin or to Harry Buxton Forman. There was no mention of the Fanny Brawne letters in the correspondence that passed between Rosa Llanos y Keats, Fanny Keats's eldest daughter, and Harry Buxton Forman, when the family decided that John's letters should go to the British Museum.

So the matter remained until 1934, when information was received that a life-long collector of Keats had bequeathed his collection of books and Keatsiana to the Keats Memorial House, Hampstead. A condition of acceptance was that the gift should be regarded as anonymous. Included in the gift were these letters, so once again after many vicissitudes they came back to the house where they had originally been written. They were at once recognized as those from which Amy Lowell had been privileged to quote a few tantalizing passages in her two-volume life of Keats. These quotations excited considerable curiosity and a certain scepticism amongst Keats enthusiasts, but no information as to the number or whereabouts of the letters was forthcoming. All that Miss Lowell could say was that 'they were the property of a gentleman who does not wish his name to be disclosed.' They have since been examined by experts, all of whom agree that their authenticity is beyond question, and that as human documents they are invaluable.

From the first letter where Fanny Brawne expresses her pleasure in complying with her lover's desire that she should write to his sister, her sympathy and compassion for the young and friendless girl of seventeen are evident. Although Severn's first letters from Rome were full of optimism for Keats's recovery, she knew within herself that never would she see him again. The tone of the early letters betrays this fear, which with a common-sense decision she makes no pretence to hide. The letter of February the 1st, 1821 (No. 6), betrays her agony of mind: 'Oh my dear, he is very ill. . . . He did not get better nor did he get worse. But could I conceal from myself that with him, not getting better was getting worse?' As hope leaves her the knowledge that she will never see him again causes her to rail against the fate that has befallen them: 'Is it to be borne that he, formed for every thing good, and, I think I dare say it, for every thing great, is to give up his hopes of life and happiness, so young too, and to be murdered, for that is the case, by the mere malignity of the world.' After the news of his death she writes to console the younger girl, telling her that she knows 'my Keats is happy, happier a thousand times than he could have been here, for Fanny,

you do not, you never can know how much he has suffered.'
She asks for her friendship and tells her that she 'must consider my Mother as more than a stranger for your brother loved her very much . . . and had he returned I should have been his wife and he would have lived with us.'

Then is shown her determination that no one shall share him with her: 'I have not mentioned your brother. To no one but you would I mention him . . . but I can tell you who next to me (I must say *next* to me) loved him best, that I have not got over it and never shall.' This attitude she maintained, and when some nine years later Brown wrote to her asking her permission to use letters and poems addressed to her in a projected life of the poet, the same reluctance is reflected in her reply. Though overwhelmed with grief she writes bravely, and despite her dislike of the Abbeys endeavours to persuade Fanny Keats to conciliate them, that her life in their society may be made more pleasant, admitting, despite her criticism of the family, that 'Abbey has acted to the best of his judgement.' She endeavours to train the young girl's mind towards a love for that which is best in literature, and sends her the journals and magazines of the day. Her own appreciation of literature and art is reflected in her remarks on the books she has read and the pictures she has seen.

These letters show Fanny Brawne, who was but twenty years of age, as a young woman of remarkable perception and imagination, keen in the observance of character and events, possessing an unusual critical faculty, and intellectually fitted to become the wife of Keats. The feelings she expresses towards the memory of Keats, confirmed by the observations of Gerald Griffin, who in a letter to his sister (July, 1826) describes her 'as beautiful, elegant and accomplished a girl as any, or more than any I have seen here,' compel the reader to repudiate the accusation of shallowness levelled against her in some quarters. Those who have believed in Fanny Brawne's devotion to Keats have the satisfaction of knowing that their faith has at last been justified.

In editing the letters I have adhered to the spelling and punctuation of the original manuscripts. Some words Fanny Brawne elected to spell as Nathan Bailey gave them in his *Etymological English Dictionary*, which Keats also used; beyond these there are but few departures from accepted orthography. To add to the readers' understanding a short biographical sketch of both Fanny Keats and Fanny Brawne is given, besides such explanatory notes as are necessary to throw light upon obscure allusions or quotations from other letters. As Keats's life and thought have been so adequately dealt with by biographers and critics, no attempt has been made to treat the letters other than as correspondence between the betrothed and the sister of the poet.

Grateful acknowledgement is made to Mrs. Oswald Ellis for permission to reprint her grandmother's letters, and also for allowing the reproduction of the portrait miniature, to Mr. Maurice Buxton Forman for his most generous help, to Mr. Edmund Blunden for valuable suggestions, and also to Mr. Lionel R. McColvin for assistance in many directions.

F.E.

Keats House, Hampstead.

September 1936.

FRANCES BRAWNE

AFTERWARDS MRS. LOUIS LINDON

FANNY BRAWNE was born at Hampstead on August the 9th, 1800, being the elder daughter of Samuel and Frances Brawne. Her father died in 1809 leaving his widow with two daughters, Frances and Margaret, and a son, Samuel. Nothing is known of Mrs. Brawne until 1818, when she became the tenant of the half of Wentworth Place belonging to Charles Brown, while he and Keats were on a walking tour in Scotland. Being neighbours of Mr. and Mrs. Charles Wentworth Dilke and the two houses having a common garden, a friendship sprang up between the families which even after Mrs. Brawne's tragic death in 1829 continued for many years. When Keats was warned by the doctor at Inverness to discontinue the tour, he returned to Hampstead, arriving in a dishevelled state on August the 18th. Calling immediately upon Mrs. Dilke to thank her for her kindness to his brother Tom, then dying of consumption in Well Walk, he was probably at once introduced to the Brawnes. The time he could spare from Tom's bedside and visiting his sister at Walthamstow was spent at Wentworth Place. His first mention of Fanny Brawne is in the journal letter of December, 1818, to his brother George in America, in which after referring to Tom's death he says that he is going to 'domesticate' with Brown. Later he writes 'Mrs. Brawne who took Brown's house for the Summer, still resides in Hampstead [she had removed to lodgings a short distance away]—she is a very nice woman—and her daughter senior is I think beautiful and elegant, graceful, silly, fashionable and strange, we have a little tiff now and then—and she behaves a little better, or I must have sheered off.' The attraction is evident, and a few days later in the same letter he draws a pen-portrait of her in which while still attacking he yet more stoutly defends. By this time he was her declared lover, and it seems probable from her remark in her letter of December, 1821 (No. 16), that Christmas Day 'three years ago was the happiest day I had ever then spent,' that it was on that day she became engaged to the poet. It is not proposed here to enlarge upon the love story of Keats and Fanny Brawne. That he worshipped her we know; that she treasured his letters and the ring he gave her we know; that she dearly loved him is proved by these letters. In whatever light we look upon Fanny Brawne the fact remains that, without her love, life would have meant but a small thing and a misery to Keats in his last years.

During the last few weeks of his life in England Keats was devotedly nursed by Fanny and her mother in their Hampstead home, and the day before he left Wentworth Place he wrote to his sister that she should have news of him from 'a friend'; that friend was, of course, Fanny Brawne, and within a week the first news of the travellers was sent to Fanny Keats at Walthamstow.

After the tragic death in November, 1829, of her mother—the 'kind lady' of whom Severn speaks so appreciatively—Fanny Brawne and her sister moved from Wentworth Place. Within two years they had suffered a double bereavement, as their only brother had died in April, 1828, at the age of 23. Orphaned and alone they left the house which now had only sad memories for them.

On June the 15th, 1833, twelve years after the death of Keats, Fanny Brawne was married at the Parish Church, St. Marylebone, to Mr. Louis Lindo, who was of Spanish extraction. Her husband afterwards changed his name to Lindon, and regarding our lack of knowledge as to how she first came to know him, it is interesting to speculate that Fanny Keats's husband, Valentine Llanos, may have brought them together. The same year Margaret Brawne married at Dieppe the Chevalier da Cunha, son of the Marquis d'Inleamprepa. Within a year Mr. and Mrs. Lindon were living at Düsseldorf, where their elder son, Herbert Brawne Lindon, was born. There were two other children of the marriage, Edmund and Margaret. For some years they moved about the Continent, and her scrap-book contains many views of the places they visited. This scrap-book and a book containing her costume plates (both presented with other valuable relics to Keats House by her granddaughter, Mrs. Oswald Ellis) give an excellent idea of her artistic taste. Filled with reproductions of the great masters, prints of beautiful buildings, and costumes of all ages, they show her to have been a woman of culture, appreciative of the beautiful in art, even as her letters provide evidence of her taste in literature. After a tranquil married life she died on December the 4th, 1865; her husband followed her seven years later. Both were buried in Brompton Cemetery.

Fanny Keats de Llanos, about 1850
identified by her grand-daughter Señorita Elena Brockman y Llanos
Madrid, November 1935

FRANCES MARY KEATS

AFTERWARDS SEÑORA VALENTINE LLANOS

FANNY KEATS was born on June the 3rd, 1803, at the 'Swan and Hoop,' Moorgate, being the youngest of the four Keats children. After the death of her mother in 1810 she was cared for by her grandmother, Mrs. Jennings, and when she died in 1814 all the children came under the guardianship of Richard Abbey, a wholesale tea and coffee merchant, and John Sandalls. Sandalls soon relinquished his authority, and Abbey, a strict and unsympathetic business man, became the sole arbiter of their destinies until they came of age. Fanny Keats was taken into his home, and by him placed in an 'academy for young ladies' at Walthamstow, conducted by Miss Tuckey and Miss Caley. We have no information about her schooldays, but she was there when, in September, 1817, Keats addresses to her from Oxford the first extant letter of their correspondence. 'Let us now begin a regular question and answer,' he writes, and after describing the legend of Endymion tells her of the family movements and asks her taste in books. From December, 1818, letters ceased to be addressed to the care of Miss Tuckey, and were sent to Mr. Abbey's either at Pancras Lane or Walthamstow. Fanny's schooldays were over, in spite of her desire to stay and John's efforts to persuade Abbey to allow her to do so. She was then fifteen.

From Keats's letters it is evident that there was little intimacy between the brothers and their sister. Abbey, annoyed with what he considered John's wasteful life, did his utmost to prevent them meeting, carrying his prejudices to what Keats considered unreasonable lengths, even objecting to her receiving letters from him. It must be remembered that, except for John, Fanny was alone. George had emigrated to America in June, 1818, and Tom had died at Hampstead in the following December. Replying to his sister's complaints Keats writes (February 27th, 1819): 'You must pay no attention to Mrs. Abbey's unfeeling and ignorant gabble.' Later, as may be seen, Fanny Brawne was of the same opinion. Such remarks, possibly seen by her guardian, added to the strained relations between him and Keats. Abbey also took exception to their calling together upon friends, and seems to have opposed even a visit by Fanny to her dying brother. 'I have seen Mr. Abbey three times about you, and have not been able to get his consent,' John told his sister in a note of November the 5th, 1818. And so it came about that Fanny Keats and Fanny Brawne did not meet until after John's death. Correspondence, however, was fairly frequent between brother and sister until Keats left England, and his last letter, written two days before his departure, dictated to and in the handwriting of Fanny

Brawne, says, 'It is not illness that prevents me from writing but as I am recommended to avoid every sort of fatigue I have accepted the assistance of a friend, who I have desired to write to you when I am gone and to communicate any intelligence she may hear of me.' This friend was Fanny Brawne, and the ensuing correspondence shows how faithfully she fulfilled his behest.

It is not known how long Fanny Keats remained with the Abbeys after she came of age, but as she was married in 1826 it is surmised that she left them soon after she attained her majority. Having no living relatives in England, and, as far as can be ascertained, few friends apart from the Dilkes and the Brawnes, her movements must of necessity have been greatly restricted. H. Buxton Forman states that she had considerable difficulty in obtaining her patrimony from Abbey, and was only successful after repeated efforts and the assistance of Charles Wentworth Dilke, who with his wife had befriended Keats and his brothers and sister since 1818.

The earliest contemporary reference to Fanny Keats's marriage to Valentine Llanos y Guiterez, generally known as Valentine Llanos, was brought to light by Mr. Blunden in 1931 when he reprinted extracts from the *Life of Gerald Griffin* (London, 1843). In June, 1825, Griffin writes that he hopes to become acquainted with the sister of Keats the poet, and goes on 'My Spanish friend, Valentine Llanos, was intimate with him, and spoke with him three days before he died.' From Letter No. 12 in this collection it may be gathered that Llanos had frequently called on the Brawnes at Wentworth Place before October, 1821, and there is the question, 'You have not I suppose seen Mr. Guiterez, he called about a fortnight ago to take leave as he intended to pass a week or two at Walthamstow.' He probably called on Fanny shortly afterwards and there can be little doubt that this was her first meeting with her future husband. They were married on March the 30th, 1826, at St. Luke's, Chelsea, where Fanny Keats had lived perhaps with, or near, the Dilkes after she left the Abbey household in 1824. Llanos was an accomplished Spanish gentleman resident in England and the author of two novels, *Don Esteban* (1825) and *Sandoval the Freemason* (1826), both published by Henry Colburn. In July, 1826, Griffin spent an evening with Llanos and his wife when Fanny Brawne was also of the party. A fortnight later he writes that they are going to France, 'which I regret as deeply as it is possible for me to say.' By 1828 they were back in England and settled at Wentworth Place as neighbours of the Brawnes, in that part of the house once occupied by Keats and Charles Brown. Griffin dined with them, and again met Fanny Brawne, whose witty conversation much impressed him.

Late in 1833 Llanos and his wife left Hampstead and returned to Spain, and after some travelling finally settled in

Madrid. There were four children of the marriage, two sons and two daughters, and Joseph Severn records meeting the family in Rome in 1861 where Señora Llanos had gone to visit her married daughter, whose husband, Count Brockmann, was Chief Engineer of the Roman Railways. In 1885 Señor Llanos died, and shortly after his widow was awarded a small Civil List pension. She died on December the 16th, 1889, at the advanced age of 86. Her surviving grandchildren, Señor Enrique Brockmann and his sister Señora Elena Brockmann, still reside at the house in Madrid where their grandparents lived for many years.

LETTERS OF
FANNY BRAWNE TO FANNY KEATS
1820–1824

Fanny Keats de Llanos
from the original portrait in oils
by her son, Don Juan Llanos y Keats

Monday afternoon
[September 18, 1820.]

My dear Miss Keats

 Your brother [1] *on leaving England expressed a wish that I should occasionally write to you;* [2] *a wish with which I feel the greatest pleasure in complying, but I cannot help thinking I require some kind of introduction, instead of which I must inform you of all my claims to your correspondence and I assure you I think them no slight ones, for I have known your brother for two years, am a great friend of Mrs Dilke's who I believe you like, and once sent you a message, which I do not know whether you received by a lady who had then never seen you but who expected to do so, a Mrs Cornish.* *Besides which I have several times invited you to stay with me during the last time your brother George was in England, an indulgence which was not granted me.* *You see I have been quite intimate with you, most likely without you ever having heard of my name.* *Besides* all *this your brother has been staying with us for the last six weeks of his being in this country and my Mother has nursed him. He left us last Wednesday but as the ship waited a few days longer than we expected, he did not sail from London till 7 o'clock yesterday morning. This afternoon we have received letters from two of his friends* [3] *who accompanied him as far as Gravesend; they both declare his health and spirits to be better than they could have expected. I do not enclose you the letters or send you all the particulars because M*r* Haslam said he should call on you very soon and he may have seen you before you receive this note; if that should not be the case, you will be pleased to hear that he went part of the way with him: his kindness cannot be described. As he was uneasy at your brother's travelling by himself he persuaded a friend* [4] *to go with him, and in a very few weeks M*r* Brown, who you probably know by name will follow him. I cannot tell you how much every one have exerted themselves for him, nor how much he is liked, which is the more wonderful as he is the last person to exert himself to gain people's friendship. I am certain he has some spell that attaches them to him, or else he has fortunately met with a set of friends that I did not believe could be found in the world. May I hope, at some time to receive a letter from you? - Perhaps you have an objection to write to a stranger. If so, I will try not to be very much disappointed* *if your objection is too strong to be overcome. For my own part I have long ceased to consider you a stranger and though this first letter may be a little stiff—because I wish to let you know what a time I have been acquainted with you, it will not be the case again, for at any rate I shall write once more whether you answer or not, as soon as letters are received from your brother, which I hope will not be for some time, for writing agitates him extremely. In Mr Haslam you will see the best person in the world to raise your spirits, he feels so certain your brother will soon recover his health. What an unconscionable* first *letter. I remain yours, allow me to say, affectionately*

Frances Brawne

Wentworth Place, Hampstead.
Monday afternoon.

POSTMARK: Sp. 19, 1820. NN.
ADDRESS: *Miss Keats,*
        Richard Abbey's Esq.
        Walthamstow.

1 Keats left Wentworth Place on Wednesday, Sept. 13th, 1820, and stayed with John Taylor in Fleet Street until he embarked on the *Maria Crowther* on the 17th. Fanny Brawne wrote her first letter to Fanny Keats the following day.
2 Keats dictated a letter to his sister (*Letters*, p. 517), dated Sept. 11th, 1820: 'It is not illness that prevents me writing, but as I am recommended to avoid

every sort of fatigue I have accepted the assistance of a friend (Fanny Brawne) who I have desired to write to you when I am gone, and to communicate any intelligence she may hear of me.' Both letter and signature are in Fanny Brawne's handwriting. The letter was written two days before he left Wentworth Place. Keats never wrote again either to his sister or his betrothed. The letters he received from them were buried with him unopened.

3 Probably John Taylor and Wm. Haslam. Taylor also wrote to Fanny Keats telling her 'On Sunday morning (the 17th. September) Mr. Keats went on board the *Maria Crowther*, for Naples, and about noon reached Gravesend. . . . Mr. Taylor, Mr. Haslam, and Mr. Woodhouse accompanied Mr. Keats to Gravesend, and left him at 4 o'clock on Sunday afternoon—He was then comfortably settled in his new habitation with every prospect of having a pleasant voyage.'

4 Joseph Severn. Brown did not go to Italy until August, 1822.

Friday night
[October 6, 1820.]

My dear Miss Keats

 First I must return you my thanks for your readiness in accepting me as a correspondent, and then hasten to inform you I have heard of your brother. I received yesterday a letter from Mrs Dilke with part of a letter from a relation[1] *of hers, copied out for my benefit, as I shall copy it for yours 'I have had some very unexpected visitors, Mr Keats and Mr Severn. They had been beating about with a contrary wind ever since they left London, and at last put into Portsmouth. I think Mr Keats much better than I expected and Mr Severn said he was sure that notwithstanding the hardships they had undergone, he was much better than when he left London.'*

 I cannot say this news pleases me much, I was in hopes that by this time he was half-way to Naples. He left Portsmouth on the 29th of September, the wind being favorable, the next day it again changed contrary to their wishes, but they did not return so it is supposed the captain put to Sea. I had a message for you from your brother before he left Hampstead as well as a lock of hair, both of which I forgot. He particularly requests you will avoid colds and coughs, and desires you never to go into the cold air out of the hothouse. The hair I myself cut off for you. It is very short, as he had little at the time. If you wish to use it in a manner that requires more pray mention it, I have some that was cut off two or three years ago I believe, and there is no difference in the color.

The Mrs Cornish I mean visits a family of the name of Goss or something like it; she told me she was frequently in the habit of calling, with them, on M^r and Mrs Abbey; but if she described her intimacy falsely, all I can say is that she is a foolish woman and if ever I see her again, I will ask her what she could mean. At any rate, her daughter, whose name is Grace, remembers you about six years ago, but she was so stupid I could make her understand nothing. My Mother is just returned from the city, and she saw Mr Haslam who had received a letter [2] from Mr Severn, not dated so late by some days as that Mrs Dilke received; Mr Keats had had no return of his complaint, and had suffered comparatively little from sea-sickness. I believe we shall receive that letter or one like it shortly. If that is the case I will send it to you or

copy it for you.   I will not make any request about a speedy
answer but leave it to your own inclinations

Your affectionate Friend

Frances Brawne

NO POSTMARK OR ADDRESS.

1 The first letter definitely fixes the date that Keats left Wentworth Place: Wednesday, the 13th of September, 1820.   This has always been in doubt (see Lowell, vol. ii, p. 460), though Colvin (p. 488) gives this date, but does not give the authority for the statement.   The *Maria Crowther* left Gravesend for Naples on Monday evening, September the 18th.   The vessel put into Portsmouth on September the 28th, and Keats visited Mr. Snook, C. W. Dilke's brother-in-law, at Bedhampton.

2 A long letter describing the miseries of the passengers as the vessel beat down channel.   (Colvin, p. 489.)

Monday Morn^g
[November 27, 1820.]

My dear Friend

  I do not know whether you will consider mine a long silence but I can assure you it has not been the effect of forgetfulness. I was staying in town at the time your letter arrived, and though I soon returned home it was only for a very few days. Besides which I thought it would be better to wait a short time in consequence of what you mentioned about Mrs Abbey. I was not quite a stranger to your situation in that family and I should write a eulogium on that lady's character in particular but that I am affraid of some unlucky accident which might expose at the same time my opinion and our correspondence. Even now I tremble at what I have said as I am ignorant whether you receive your letters in public or whether you have private arrangements for that purpose.

  We received a letter[1] *from your brother about a fortnight ago. So I dare say did you. I was so extremely happy to hear of his arrival at Naples, that I overlooked*

10

the hardships of their wretched voyage and even the bad spirits he wrote in. The weather was so much against him, joined to his spirits, which prey on him and continually make him worse, that it would have been too much to expect any great improvement in his health. He mentioned that Mr Severn was writing to Mr Haslam [2] and that we should have the letter to read, as it would give a better account of him than he could write himself. However we have not yet received it. When it arrives, I will copy any material part for you. I promised to do so before, when I received a former letter [3] of Mr Severn's which arrived while I was in London. It was dated a day or two before their stay at Portsmouth and said your brother was a little better and that his spirits were good, which I think most material.

I saw that unlucky Mrs Cornish [4] a short time before I received your last letter. By way of saying something I began to talk about you. Of course I did not tell her she had been suspected as an impostor, but I talked as carelessly as if our acquaintance had been formed on Mrs Abbey's recommendation. When I read your letter I was sorry for what I had done, so if I see her again I mean to insist that her ears have deceived her and that I did not say I had heard from you but of you from your brother. Not that I expect her to remember a word about it, or even that *either of us exists. She said she was soon going to stay with Mrs Goss and that she should most likely call with her on* your *family.*

I saw Mrs Dilke the other day and delivered your message. She desires me to return her love. My Mother with an elderly lady's decorum begs to be remembered to you (and I beg for the future that you will always take it for granted she does so, as I am apt to forget her messages) and I send you my most affectionate love

Frances Brawne

POSTMARK: Hampstead 7 o'clock, Nov. 27, 1820. NT.
ADDRESS: *For Miss Keats,*
    Richard Abbeys Esq.
    Walthamstow.
WRITTEN INSIDE COVER: *Wentworth Place Novr.* 27 [1820.]

1 Written to Mrs. Brawne from Naples Harbour, Oct. 24th, 1820. (*Letters,* p. 522.) It ends 'Goodbye Fanny. God bless you.'
On Wednesday, Nov. 1st, 1820, Severn wrote from Naples to his sister Maria: 'I have arrived here in perfect health, much of it gained in this sea voyage, . . . O that I could say all this of poor Keats, he suffered most severely— many times I have expected him to die—but at present in this city he is better—most certainly here is hope of his recovery—I still think to bring him back well—It is a source of the greatest consolation that I am with him.'
2 A long letter from Naples, Nov. 1st–2nd, 1820, to Wm. Haslam describing the miseries of the voyage. (Colvin, pp. 498–500.)
3 Severn's journal letter to Haslam, Sept. 19th, 1820. (Colvin, pp. 489–90.)
4 Mrs. Goss and Mrs. Cornish. Friends of the Abbeys, Dilkes, and Brawnes. But nothing further is known about them.

Monday afternoon
[December 4, 1820.]

My dear Girl

 I am really affraid you will think me a most trouble-
some correspondent but this time I do not write on my own
account but by your brothers wish. Mr Brown has received
a letter from him dated November the 2nd ¹ from which I
find he has not yet written to you, as he wished someone
to do it for him. In the letter we received before dated the
24th of October, he said they had to stay on board ten days
longer to perform Quarantine. So far they had had a
tolerable voyage from the time they left Portsmouth. He
did not think himself better or worse but his spirits were
not very good. When he wrote to Mr Brown they were just
arrived on shore, their sufferings during the quarantine were
beyond any thing we can imagine. From your brother I
never expect a very good account, but you may imagine how
lowering to the spirits it must have been when Mr Severn
who I never imagined it was possible for any thing to make
unhappy, who I never saw for ten minutes serious, says he

13

was so overcome that he was obliged to relieve himself by shedding tears.[2] He however says your brother was a little recovered, at least quite as much so as he could expect, the day after his arrival. He says, if he can but get his spirits good, he will answer for his being well in a moderate time; which shows he does not consider he has any complaint of consequence. They had met with several friends who were extremely kind to them, particularly the brother of a young lady a passenger with them,[3] who went out in dreadful health, and who, God knows, I have a thousand times wished at the bottom of the sea as I know she made it worse for your brother. The Physician[4] to whom our friends were recommended was at Rome when they reached Naples and they had made up their minds to go to Rome. I have written to him today and directed the letter there.[5] If you would like to write to him mention it, and I will get the direction, for I cannot give it you now as it is a foreign one and I should make some mistake so I will ask Mr Brown again when I see him. I should like to have given you a better account but I must say that considering all things it is as well as we could have expected. My dear you must not consider this a letter from me but from your brother, for I should be quite ashamed not to mention being frightened of an acquaintance of yours—a letter has been

*received from Mrs George Keats to her brother. They are
all very well and you may by this time expect another little
nephew or niece* 6

Yours very affectionately

Frances B——

Monday afternoon

POSTMARK: Hampstead. 4 o'clock Dec. 5. 1820. ev.
ADDRESS: *Miss Keats,*

      Richard Abbeys Esq.

      Walthamstow.

1 This is the letter in which Keats begs Brown 'For my sake, be her advocate for ever.' Naples, Nov. 1st, 1820. (*Letters*, p. 523.)
2 Severn to Haslam, Naples, Nov. 1st, 1820. 'For myself I have stood it firmly until this morning when in a moment my spirits dropped at the sight of his suffering—a plentiful shower of tears (which he did not see) has relieved me somewhat.' (Colvin, p. 498.)
3 Mr. Charles Cotterell, brother of Miss Cotterell who was a passenger (and a consumptive) on the *Maria Crowther*.
4 Dr. (afterwards Sir) James Clark, who attended Keats in Rome. He arranged the lodgings for Keats and Severn in Rome in the Piazza di Spagna, the house being opposite his own.
5 Keats never opened any of Fanny Brawne's or Fanny Keats's letters; they were buried with him.
6 George Keats wrote to his sister from Louisville, Kentucky, January, 1821, 'You have now my dear Fanny another niece, she was born on the 18th. December [1820].' This was Rosalind, who predeceased her father. (*Letters*, p. 515.)

[January 15, 1821.]

My dear Miss Keats

    I am almost ashamed to write to you though I have been waiting for above three weeks to do so, but I hope you will forgive me, for it is not quite *my fault. On the* 23rd *of December, Mr Brown received a letter from your brother in which he desired that someone would write to you,*[1] *to say he was as well as he could expect, and that we should hear from him in a few days. This letter I waited for some time, but as we have received since that a letter from Mr Severn, in which no mention is made of it I conclude he changed his mind fearful that the exertion might fatigue him. When Mr Severn wrote, they were in Rome after a most wretched journey. They lodged opposite an English Physician*[2] *to whom they were recommended, and who paid them the greatest attention. Your brother went out on horseback every day.*[3] *I am extremely glad they have chosen Rome instead of Naples for their winter residence. I am sure the climate is far preferable besides the disturbed state Naples seems likely to be in, and which*

My dear Miss Keah

I am almost
ashamed to write to you though
I have been waiting for above three
weeks to do so, but I hope you will
forgive me, for it is not quite my
fault. On the 23rd of December, Mr
Brown received a letter from your
brother in which he desired that
someone would write to you, to say

her was as well he could expect,
that we should hear from him in
few days. This letter I waited for
time but as we have received,
that a letter from M.r Severn, in
no mention is made of it I once
he changed his mind fearful that
the exertion might fatigue him.
when M.r Severn wrote, they were
Rome after a most wretched jour
they lodged opposite an English P
cian to whom they were recommend

d who paid them the greatest
ntion. Your brother went out on
rseback every day. I am extremely
d they have chosen Rome instead
Naples for their winter residence.
 one the climate is far preferable
ides the disturbed state Naples
ns likely to be in, and which no
bt induced them to quit it.

, my dear Girl, if you have any
telligence of them, let me know it.

however trifling we shall feel it,
the greatest consequence. The ~
is so long before either party can
receive letters, that it makes me
very impatient. My Mother ~
her best remembrance to you, a
believe me to remain

Yours most affectionately

Francis Brawne

Monday Morn—

no doubt induced them to quit it. Do, my dear Girl, if you have any intelligence of them, let me know it, however trifling we shall feel it of the greatest consequence. The time is so long before either party can receive letters, that it makes me very impatient. My Mother desires her best remembrances to you, and believe me to remain

Yours most affectionately

Frances Brawne

Monday Morn^g.

POSTMARK: Hampstead, Jan. 16. 1821.
WRITTEN INSIDE COVER IN PENCIL IN FANNY KEATS'S HAND—
 '*Tuesday*,
  Rabbits Tuesday,
   January 16th 1821.'

---

1 Probably the last letter he wrote. Rome, Nov. 30th, 1820. 'I have an habitual feeling of my real life having passed, and that I am leading a posthumous existence. . . . Write to George as soon as you receive this, and tell him how I am, as far as you can guess; and also a note to my sister—who walks about my imagination like a ghost—she is so like Tom. I can scarcely bid you goodbye, even in a letter. I always made an awkward bow.' (*Letters*, p.525.)

2 Dr. (afterwards Sir) James Clark, Piazza di Spagna.

3 'Yet I ride the little horse' he wrote in the letter quoted in note 1, above.

17

February 1st Hampstead.
[1821.]

My dear Girl

I have been this week wishing to write to you but putting it off every day in hopes of having something concerning your brother to communicate which would not give you pain, but it is in vain to wait any longer. Oh my dear, he is very ill, he has been so ever since the 8th of December. If I had written this letter two hours sooner I should have owned to you that I had scarcely a hope remaining and even now when I have just received a letter from Mr Severn with the nearest approaching to good news that we have had since this last attack, there is nothing to rest upon, merely a hope, a chance. But I will tell you all in as collected a way as I can. On the 10th of Jany Mr Brown received a letter from Rome saying your brother had been attacked with spitting of blood and that the symptoms were very bad. He had been ill for 17 days and did not appear to get better. I judged of you by myself and though I was then about to write I deferred it for some

18

*time in hopes a letter more cheering might arrive. I
cannot think I was wrong. If you knew how much I re-
gretted that it had not been kept from me* [1] *—how continually I thought a fortnight or even a weeks ignorance of
it would have been more pain spared—and when at last I
could not bear to keep silence any longer for fear you should
fancy the least neglect should have occasioned it, I wrote
a letter that without mentioning any thing positively bad,
did not, if I may judge from your answer give you hopes
of a speedy recovery. Once or twice we have heard slight
accounts, which were neither calculated to raise or depress
our hopes but yesterday I was told of a letter from the
Physician* [2] *which said he was exactly the same. He did
not get better nor did he get worse. But could I conceal
from myself that with him, not getting better was getting
worse? If ever I gave up hope, I gave it up then. I tried
to destroy it, I tried to persuade myself that I should never
see him again. I felt that you ought no longer to remain
in ignorance and the whole of this day I have been thinking
how I could tell you. I am glad, very glad, I waited, for
I have just received the account I spoke of in the beginning
of this letter. Mr Severn says that for the first time he
feels a hope,* [3] *he thinks he shall bring him back to us.
Surely, that is saying a great deal—and yet the reason he*

19

gives for that hope destroys it, for the last 3 days (the letter was dated the 11th of Jan) your brother had been calm, he had resigned himself to die. Oh can you bear to think of it, he has given up even wishing to live—Good God! is it to be borne that he, formed for every thing good, and, I think I dare say it, for every thing great, is to give up his hopes of life and happiness, so young too, and to be murdered, for that is the case, by the mere malignity of the world, joined to want of feeling in those who ought above all to have felt for him—I am sure nothing during his long illness has hurt me so much as to hear he was resigned to die. But I will say no more about it. In a week or ten days I will enclose you the letter. You should have it sooner but we are obliged, in consequence of a message respecting money to send it to a friend in London first.[4] And now my dear Girl, my dear Sister for so I feel you to be, forgive me if I have not sufficiently softened this wretched news. Indeed I am not now able to contrive words that would appear less harsh—If I am to lose him I lose every thing and then you, after my Mother will be the only person I shall feel interest or attachment for—I feel that I love his sister as my own—God Bless you, he has talked of you continually, he did so when he was in great danger last spring.[5] He has also expressed a wish for my Mother *and Mrs Dilke to call and see you.*[6]   *I cannot give up a hope that you may one day come and see me.*   *Do you think Mr Abby will ever be induced to give his consent.*   *If you think so whenever you write, tell me, and my Mother should ask his permission, but not just at present unless you think that would not be venturing too far at first.—*

I remain my dearest Girl
Yours very affectionately

Fanny

I forgot to mention he reads no letters for fear of agitating himself—I know I may trust to you never to mention me either now—or at any future time as connected with your brother[7]*—as I know he would dislike that sort of gossiping way in which people not concerned mention those things*[8]*—God bless you once more—*

POSTMARK: 12 o'clock Feb. 2. 1821. Ev.
ADDRESS: *Miss Keats*
       Richard Abby's Esqre.
       Walthamstow

1 Letter from Brown to Severn, mid-January, 1821: 'Miss Brawne does not actually know there is no hope, she looks more sad every day. She has insisted on writing to him by this post, take care of the letter—if too late, let it be returned unopened . . . to Mrs. Brawne.'
2 Letter from Dr. Clark, Rome, Jan. 3rd, 1821. 'The state of his mind is the worst possible for one in his condition, and will undoubtedly hurry on an event that I fear is not far distant.'

3 Letter from Severn to Mrs. Brawne, Rome, Jan. 11th, 1821. After writing that 'I most certainly think that I shall bring him back to England . . .' Severn continues: 'He has now given up all thoughts, hopes, or even wish for recovery. His mind is in a state of peace for the final leave he has taken of this world and all its future hopes. . . .' After describing his anxieties, he sends his compliments to Miss Brawne, and concludes: 'O! I would my unfortunate friend had never left your Wentworth Place—for the hopeless advantages of this comfortless Italy. He has many, many times talked over "the few happy days at your house, the only time when his mind was at ease".'

4 The friend was John Taylor. There was a misunderstanding over the payment of money to Keats through the Roman banker Torlonia. On receipt of this letter Taylor (who had advanced the money for Keats's use) took immediate steps for the drafts to be honoured on presentation.

5 The first severe haemorrhage and illness, February, 1820.

6 Letter from Severn to Brown, Rome, Dec. 14th, 1820. After describing Keats's sufferings as his life slowly passed to its close he says: 'I heard Keats say how he should like Mrs. Brawne and Mrs. Dilke to visit his sister at Walthamstow—will you say this for me.'

7 This final paragraph shows how strongly Fanny Brawne regarded her betrothal to Keats as entirely a personal matter. Her draft reply to Brown's request (*Letters*, p. lxii) nearly nine years later (Dec. 1829), for permission to use poems and letters addressed to her by Keats expresses the same conviction. See also letter No. 9.

8 See note 7, above.

Monday Morn
[February 26, 1821.]

My dear Fanny

    I enclose you the letter [1] *I promised you but I cannot send with it any news that would give you pleasure. A letter has been received, which I have not seen dated the* 25th *he was not worse but he was not better, and faint as are the hopes M*r *Severn gives I dare not think them well founded. All I do is to persuade myself, I shall never see him again—but I will not say any more perhaps it may afford you more comfort to hope for the best. God bless you my dearest girl in a week or a fortnight I will write to you again unless I hear from Italy, should that be the case you shall be immediately informed of it.*

              Yours very affectionately

                    Frances Brawne

POSTMARK: 26 Feb. 1821. 2 o'clock.
ADDRESS: *Miss Keats*
        at Mr. Abby's
           Pancras Lane

1 Colvin's *Life of Keats*, pp. 514 et seq. 'The letters written by Severn . . . were handed round and eagerly scanned among the circle. Brown, when they came into his hands, used to read passages from them at his discretion to the Brawne ladies next door, keeping the darkest from the daughter at her mother's wish. Mrs. Brawne, evidently believing the child's heart to be deeply engaged dealt in the same manner with Severn's letters to herself. The girl seems to have divined none the less that her lover's condition was past hope, and her demeanour . . . to have been human and natural. Keats, writes Brown in a broken style,—"is present to me everywhere and at all times . . . Much as I have loved him, I never knew how closely he was wound about my heart. Mrs. Brawne was greatly agitated when I told her of—and her daughter—I don't know how—for I was not present—yet she bears it with great firmness, mournfully and without affectation. I understand she says to her mother, 'I believe he must soon die, and when you hear of his death, tell me immediately. I am not a fool.'"' Colvin continues, 'We hear in the meantime of her being in close correspondence with his sister Fanny at Walthamstow. When the news of the end came, Brown writes,—"I felt at the moment utterly unprepared for it. Then *she*—she was to have it told to her, and the worst had been concealed from her knowledge ever since your [Severn's] December letter. It is now five days since she heard it. I shall not speak of the first shock, nor of the following days,—it is enough she is now pretty well—and thro'out she has shown a firmness of mind which I little expected from one so young, and under such a load of grief."'

Tuesday Afternoon
[March 27, 1821.]

You will forgive me, I am sure, my dear Fanny, that I did not write to you before, I could not for my own sake and I would not for yours, as it was better you should be prepared for what, even knowing as much as you did, you could not expect[1]—*I should like to hear that you my dearest Sister are well, for myself, I am patient, resigned, very resigned. I know my Keats is happy, happier a thousand times than he could have been here, for Fanny, you do not, you never can know how much he has suffered. So much that I do believe, were it in my power I would not bring him back. All that grieves me now is that I was not with him, and so near it as I was. Some day my dear girl I will tell you the reason and give you additional cause to hate those who should have been his friends, and yet it was a great deal through his kindness for me for he foresaw what would happen, he at least was never deceived about his complaint, though the Doctors were ignorant and unfeeling enough to send him to that wretched country to die, for it is now known that his recovery was impossible*

25

before he left us, and he might have died here with so many friends to soothe him and me me *with him. All we have to console ourselves with is the great joy he felt that all his misfortunes were at an end. At the very last he said 'I am dying thank God the time is come,'*[2] *and in a letter from M*ʳ *Severn written about a fortnight before he died*[3] *and which was not shown me, so that I thought he would live months at least if he did not recover he says 'he is still alive & calm, if I say more it will be too much, yet at times I have thought him better but he would not hear of it, the thought of recovery is beyond every thing dreadful to him—we now dare not perceive any improvement for the hope of death seems his only comfort, he talks of the quiet grave as the first rest he can ever have'—In that letter he mentions that he had given directions how he would be buried, the purse you sent him and your last letter (which he never read, for he would never open either your letters or mine after he left England) with some hair, I believe of mine, he desired to be placed in his coffin.*[4] *The truth is I cannot very well go on at present with this, another time I will tell you more—what I wish to say now relates to yourself, my Mother is coming to see you very soon. If you are in Pancrass lane she will call next Friday, that is if it be not disagreable to M*ʳ *Abby.*[5] *Do you think* *he would allow you to stay with us a short time? I have desired my Mother to ask him, though I do not know how she will prevail on herself to do it, for she is affraid of him, but Mrs Dilke will be with her to give her courage— And now my dear I must hope you will favor me with your company, it will I assure you be a real favor. And yet I hardly like to press you to make such a dull visit. I once hoped for a very different one from you, I used to anticipate the pleasure I should feel in showing every kindness and attention in my power to you. And I felt so happy when he desired me to write to you while he was away. I little thought how it would turn out. I have just recollected that perhaps you will not wish to come out so soon. Fix your own time my dear, only come. Will you have the kindness to write to me, by return of post, if you can, to say if Friday will be too soon for you to see my Mother, and if you will come, and when. I ask you with more confidence though there is little or nothing to amuse with us, because I have heard you lead a very dull life in Mr Abbys family—but we will do as much as we can to amuse you and to prevent your thinking of any thing to make you unhappy. You must consider my Mother as more than a stranger for your brother loved her very much, and used often to wish she could go with him, and had he re-*

27

turned I should have been his wife and he would have lived with us.[6] All all now in vain—could we have foreseen—but he did foresee and every one thought it was only his habit of looking for the worst—Though you are the only person in the world I wish to see, I will own I do not expect it. Your Guardian is said to be so much more than strict, and was so particular in refusing to let your brothers take you out, that I have not the least hope, but as much as we can do shall, with your consent, be tried and if it is in vain I will, before you leave London, call on you—If Mr Abby should so far think of it to ask who we are, you may if you like say my Mother is a widow and has two children besides me, both very young—send me an answer as soon as you can conveniently—My mother desires her love to you and I send a thousand good wishes to my dear sister God bless her

Frances Brawne

I have recollected that perhaps you are in the country and will not have time to write so I will say Monday next for my Mother to see you instead of Friday—Should the

28

day be Wet, tuesday will be better and so on till the first
fine day unless you are other-wise engaged which you must
let me know.

POSTMARK: Camden Town, 28 Mar. 1821.
ADDRESS: *For Miss Keats,*
    at Mr. Abbys
     Pancras Lane
      London.

1 Keats died in Rome on Feb. 23rd, 1821, and three days later was buried in the Protestant Cemetery, his epitaph being of his own choosing, 'Here lies one whose name was writ in water.'
2 Letter from Severn to Brown written soon after Keats's death, but never sent. (Colvin, p.512.)
3 Letter from Severn to Mrs. Brawne, Rome, Feb. 12th, 1821.
4 Letter from Severn to Mrs. Brawne, Rome, Feb. 12th, 1821.
5 Letter from Brown to Severn. 'I wrote to Haslam to call on Abbey, and if Abbey will permit it, Mrs. Brawne and Mrs. Dilke will call on Miss Keats. They are in mourning next door.' March 23rd, 1821.
6 This is the first intimation we have that had Keats recovered future arrangements had been made for their marriage.

Hampstead, May 23, 1821.

My dear Fanny

I find by my pocket book it is above 3 weeks since I received your letter and I am affraid you must have thought me neglectful in not writing before but as I have been staying that time in London and wished, when I did write to mention several things, I put it off till I should be by myself at home—In the first place only think of that M[rs] Abbey after her promises to my Mother behaving as she has done. Not that I expected any thing better from her. Oh my dear, what a woman for a girl to be brought up with—The description I have had of her manners and conversation has quite shocked me. For you to look forward to 3 years more of it is dreadful—I find from my Mother that M[rs] Dilke was foolish enough to mention me to her in the way I so much wished to avoid, but she appeared to know it[2] already and my Mother suspects from other things that passed, that she has read some of our letters. Do you think it possible, that she or any one of the family could get at them? You must know best, if

you are sure it could not be the case I shall know my
Mother was mistaken and that Mrs A. must have obtained
her knowledge by some other means for you see she was
better acquainted with Mrs Cornish than you supposed, indeed I should not have mentioned it at all but to put you
on your guard. Should my opinion of her ever come to her
ears she would prevent all intercourse between us, and really
I could hardly blame her for so doing. When you write
mention some day for your being in town with the hour
you are sure of Mr Abbey being at home and I will try
what I can do with him. If there is any better plan you
can think of, if it would be better to call on Mr Abbey
when you are not in town I will do that. I wish you more
than ever to be with me were it but for a short time which
it shall not be if I can persuade him to any thing. Do you
not think my dear, a little complaisance or civility on your
part might do something. But perhaps you dare not sound
him on the subject and if it would be very unpleasant to
you do not attempt it, at all events I shall wait for your
letter before I do any thing. I thought when I began to
write that I had a great deal to say and now I find I have
half filled this letter without a word of what I had intended. I have not mentioned your brother. To no one
but you would I mention him. I will suffer no one but

31

*you to speak to me of him. They are too uninterested in him to have any right to mention what is to you & me, so great a loss. I have copied a letter from Mr Severn giving an account of the last days of his life.*³ *No one knows I have it but you, and I had not sealed it up, as I thought you might wish to see it, but if you do, you must prepare for great pain, if you would rather not make yourself again unhappy, do not read it. I think you will be wise. It took me a long time to write. I have not looked at it since, nor do I mean to do so at present, but I mention it to you because though it gives pain, it also gives a certain kind of pleasure in letting us know how glad he was to die at the last. Dear Fanny, no one but you can feel with me—All his friends have forgotten him, they have got over the first shock, and that with them is all. They think I have done the same, which I do not wonder at, for I [have] taken care never to trouble them with any feelings of mine, but I can tell you who next to me (I must say* next to me) *loved him best, that I have not got over it and never shall— It's better for me that I should not forget him but not for you, you have other things to look forward to—and I would not have said any thing about him for I was affraid of distressing you but I did not like to write to you without telling you how I felt about him and leaving it to you*

3²

whether the subject should be mentioned in our letters—In a letter you sent me some time ago you mentioned your brother George in a manner that made me think you had been mislead about him. He is no favorite of mine and he never liked me so that I am not likely to say too much in his favor from affection for him, but I must say I think he is more blamed than he should be. I think him extravagant and selfish but people in their great zeal make him out much worse than that—Soon after your brother Tom died, my dear John wrote to him offering him any assistance or money in his power. At that time he was not engaged to me and having just lost one brother felt all his affection turned towards the one that remained—George I dare say at first had no thoughts of accepting his offers but when his affairs did not succeed and he had a wife and one child to support, with the prospect of another, I cannot wonder that he should consider them first and as he could not get what he wanted without coming to England he unfortunately came—By that time your brother wished to marry himself, but he could not refuse the money. It may appear very bad in George to leave him 60 pounds when he owed 80, but he had many reasons to suppose the inconvenience would not last long. Your brother had a book of poems nearly ready to come out (which his illness kept back till the summer) he had a tragedy which Mr Brown calculated his share of would be about two hundred pounds and he was writing a story which had he lived to finish would if the others failed make up for it⁴ at least so every one imagined.—George could not forsee his illness—He might be a cause of the dreadful consequences but surely a very indirect and accidental one. At the same time I cannot defend him, lately his behaviour has been very selfish and I may say shuffling. As to his returning the money I don't believe he has ever had it in his power to return a farthing or ever will have, that may not be his fault. The person who suffered most never thought so very badly of it, he used to say, 'George ought not to have done this he should have recollected that I wish to marry myself—but I suppose having a family to provide for makes a man selfish'—They tell me that latterly he thought worse of George, but I own I do not believe it —One thing is against him. I don't think he could ever have supposed it would be in his power to return the money, at the best not for many years—his brother never expected it at all, he always said he would not succeed—If when I write again I think of any thing for or against him I shall mention it—For I wish at any rate to put you on your guard—I have said I think him selfish—and I am affraid whenever you have your money in your own power

34

you will find him troublesome but my dear girl be very cautious—be warned by what has already happened—and remember he is extravagant at least every one says so. I don't know whether you will be able to connect and read all this—write as soon as you can—ever your affectionate sister & friend—

Fanny

POSTMARK: 4 o'clock. 21 My. 1821. Ev.[5]
ADDRESS: *For Miss Keats,*
        Richard Abbey's Esq.,
           Walthamstow,
             Essex.

1 This letter is of great importance. In it Fanny Brawne bares her heart and mind on her feelings towards Keats.
2 Evidently as engaged to Keats.
3 See Fanny Brawne's copy of Severn's letter to John Taylor, below.
4 *Lamia, Isabella, the Eve of St. Agnes, and other poems*, 1820. The tragedy was *Otho the Great.* The 'story' may have been *The Cap and Bells.*
5 Fanny Brawne made a mistake of two days in the date, 23rd instead of 21st.

Extract copied by Fanny Brawne from a letter of Joseph Severn to John Taylor, Apr. 16th, 1821. The original letter is in the Amy Lowell Collection at Harvard College Library, and is partly quoted in her *John Keats*, ii. 528.

'*Four days previous to his death—the change was so great that I passed each moment in dread, not knowing what the next would have—He was calm and firm at its approaches—to a most astonishing degree—He told me not to tremble for he did not think that he should be convulsed —he said "did you ever see any one die?" "no" "well then I pity you, poor Severn. What trouble and danger you have got into for me—now you must be firm for it will not last long. I shall soon be laid in the quiet grave—O! I can feel the cold earth upon me—The daisies growing over me —O for this quiet—it will be my first"—When the morning light came and still found him alive how bitterly he grieved—I cannot bear his cries—Each day he would look up in the Doctor's face to discover how long he should live he would say "how long will this posthumous life of mine* last" that look was more than we could ever bear. The extreme brightness of his eyes with his poor pallid face were not earthly—

'These four nights I watched him, each night expecting his death—on the 5th day the Doctor prepared me for it. At 4 o'clock in the afternoon the poor fellow bade me lift him up in bed—he breathed with great difficulty and seemed to lose the power of coughing up the phlegm, an immense sweat came over him so that my breath felt cold to him. "Don't breathe on me it comes like ice" he clasped my hand very fast as I held him in my arms. The phlegm rattled in his throat, it increased but still he seemed without pain, he looked upon me with extreme sensibility but without pain, at 11 he died in my arms.'

MARKED ON OUTSIDE '2. *From Mr. Severn. April* 16th'

Wednesday
[June 20, 1821.]

My dear Fanny

 I should have written to you a week ago but I waited to see if any thing could be done towards M^r or Mrs Abbeys good opinion. How little we know what we may one day come to. If any one could have told me, a year ago that I should ever be angling for Mr Abbeys good opinion, I should have been surprized—Miss Robinson is so seldom in town that I am obliged to wait weeks, before I can get hold of her, but today I went with her to call on Mrs Cornish to whom I gave a pressing invitation to come and see me at Hampstead. Miss Robinson knows my reason for wishing her acquaintance and has promised to bring her some evening to drink tea which I hope will take place before she visits Walthamstow where, though she has a pressing invitation she cannot go at present as she has a great wash coming. God help us! great washes, no doubt take place in other families but are never mentioned in company—And now my dear make the most of her if

38

you see her. I am told she is very good natured. Of course we must be careful not to let her know our reasons for courting her so much—Miss Rowcroft is the name of my other friend through whom perhaps something might be done by the Whitehursts, but though I am sure she would do anything in her power, I do not like to say any thing to her about it. Miss Robinson has offered her services and is almost as much interested in the cause as I am, she is very intimate with Mrs Whitehurst and I have no doubt will mention it to her, but Miss Rowcroft I believe knows Mrs Goss and perhaps you can make some use of her name —It is unlucky that the Goss's have lately moved farther from you it may make you less intimate [1]—

God bless you my dearest girl I have written a short note but I came from town very late and tomorrow am going early to stay with Mrs Dilke so if you write to me within the week direct to No. 5, Great Smith Street Westminster once more

God bless you dear Fanny

Frances B——

Tell me when you write what is Mrs Abbeys opinion of Mrs Cornish—

POSTMARK: Hampstead, Ju. 21. 1821. Ev.
ADDRESS: *For Miss Keats*
        Richard Abbeys Esq.
        Walthamstow

1 Apparently the persons mentioned are to be used as advocates for more freedom of movement for Fanny Keats. Miss Caroline Robinson is the only one of whom anything is known. She is the lady whom Keats mentions in the letter of December, 1818, to George, 'Miss B. thinks her a paragon of fashion.' Later she married James Ellis, and became the mother of Robinson Ellis in 1834. (*Letters*, p. 254, note.)

Letter undated [August–September, 1821.]

My dear Fanny

 I have been expecting some account of the pleasure I think you must have felt at King Lear though in it you did not see Kean to the best advantage and though the play itself is spoiled. I have only seen Miss Edmiston[1] *in Lady Macbeth and admired her person but did not think much of her acting, in Cordelia she may be better. I should have liked to have met you at the playhouse but I had both M*ʳˢ *Dilke and a cousin staying with me besides which there might not have been room in your box and to sit at any distance from you would have defeated the purpose for which I should have gone, for the play itself is not one I should wish to see again, read it as originally written and you will soon see the difference. They say as a foolish reason for acting it in its present state that formerly it was too affecting, but I am convinced that the more people are affected the more they are pleased. Perhaps you may have heard that Doctor Johnson who saw it before the alteration said it was too much to bear and that nothing should*

41

induce him to sit it out again.[2]*—I am presuming that you have not read King Lear for I think you told me you had read nothing of Shakespeare's. Mr. Brown desired me to give you his compliments and to tell you that he has a large bible and prayer book which belonged to your grandmother which, if you like to have, he will send by the carrier, he considers them as a sort of family relic and that you have the best right to them.—I think in one of your letters you said you should like to take opium but for the terrible penalty attending it, but I do not see why that should be a hindrance for it was only caused by the abuse of it. So take it—if you can.—For my part I find but one obstacle, one, to be sure that I cannot conquer; which is the taste is so dreadfully disagreable that* I *who have only a* decent *resolution for taking physic, cannot go into a room where laudenum has been, without feeling—poorly. Not that I ever tried to swallow it for pleasure but toothaches will make you sufficiently acquainted with the beautiful flavour, to* me *the idea of drinking salts or senna to produce a pleasant feeling is a very* odd *idea. I hope next time you go to the play, it will be to see Richard the third or Othello, then I think you will go out of your mind with pleasure. I never will write on half a sheet of paper again.*

*I am sure my writing is not intelligible enough to make
crossing pleasant to those who have to read it.*

Yours my dear Fanny very affectionately

F B—

Friday Night

NO ADDRESS OR POSTMARK.

1 Extract from *Edmund Kean*, by H. N. Hildebrand, 1933 (Columbia Univ. Press,
  N.Y.): 'The season of 1821–1822, at least on the tragic side, was a poor thing.
  Elliston had done nothing to strengthen the Company, save for the introduc-
  tion of a certain Miss Edmiston, who was a good find, and who with the
  veteran Mrs. West gave respectability to the female side.'
2 Fanny Brawne is shown in a new light in this letter, as a critic of the drama.
  She was probably thinking of Johnson's critique of *Lear* in Keats's 1814
  Shakespeare: 'If my sensations could add anything to the general suffrage,
  I might relate, I was many years ago so shocked by Cordelia's death, that I
  know not whether I ever endured to read again the last scenes of the play,
  till I undertook to revise them as an editor.'

43

Monday Oct^{br} 8th

My dear Fanny

If I am not mistaken this is about the time you expected to be in London—I hope you will not forget to appoint some day for my seeing you. Unless your time is very short I will not come should the day you mention prove wet but wait till the next and so on, for I need not say how I hate sloppy weather and at present there is no fixing on a day with any confidence—

Mrs Dilke is in town and expressed a great wish to accompany me whenever I paid you a visit but I am not sure that I can arrange it so as to bring her next time. I hope you have kept yourself safe from all colds, for though early to begin I have got a very disfiguring one, no doubt through my boast to Mrs Abbey that I never on any occasion caught cold. You have not I suppose seen Mr Guiterez,[1] he called about a fortnight ago to take leave as he intended to pass a week or two at Walthamstow with his friend, Mr Wigram[2] I think was the beautiful name. I would have sent a letter to you by him but men are so stupid I

was affraid of his losing it, besides thinking it very likely
you might not meet.   God bless you my dear Fanny I shall
expect every day to hear from you

Yours very affectionately

Frances Brawne

POSTMARK: Hampstead, 4 o'clock, Oct. 8. 1821. Ev.
ADDRESS: *For Miss Keats*
Richard Abbey's Esquire
Walthamstow

1 This is the first mention of Valentine Maria Llanos y Guiterez, afterwards
  known as Valentine Llanos, who was married to Fanny Keats in 1826.
  According to Gerald Griffin he knew Keats in Rome, and came to England
  shortly after the poet's death, possibly with an introduction from Severn
  to Brown and Mrs. Brawne. From the letter it is evident that Llanos had
  often called at Wentworth Place before October.
2 One of the twenty-three children of Sir Robert Wigram (1744–1830) who
  owned Walthamstow House. (*Letters* LIX–LX.)

[Undated. Late 1821.]

My dear Fanny

*I have almost changed my mind about visiting you
at Walthamstow. I think I will wait till you come to
town, which will not be above 3 or 4 weeks now. Mrs Abbey
would certainly stare and think it rather presuming on her
good nature, indeed I would rather have walked in the
fields with you than have entered her house. I assure you
she did not impose on me with all her concern for our thin
shoes and damp feet. Her appearance surprized me. I
expected a more portly redfaced dame. She is much more
in the motherly-nursey stile than I expected. Guiterez dined
with us yesterday and told me he had seen an acquaintance
of mine. After guessing for an hour to no purpose, for
though I thought of you it seemed so improbable I did not
mention it, my Mother found out; of course we laughed
at him finely for his polite offer of calling on you.¹ However I have informed him your guardian is particular and
cautioned him against letting the family see you are acquainted. Don Valentine Maria Llanos Guiterez is a*

46

pretty name, is it not? he himself is everything that a Span-ish Cavalier ought to be. You need not be affraid of speak-ing to him for he is extremely gentlemanly and well behaved. My Mother has received a letter from Mr Severn but I did not wish to read it. Did you tell Guiterez you had seen a gentleman from Italy? If so, I suppose Mr Ewing has called on you.[2] My Mother thinks it probable but I imagine it his mistake—I have only seen Mr Ewing for a few min-utes almost in the dark but he seemed so fluttered and con-fused that I could make nothing of him; but he has claims on us both from his great kindness in Italy. God bless you my dear Fanny.

Frances Brawne

Monday Morn^g.

NO ADDRESS OR POSTMARK.

1 This remark indicates that Llanos was introduced to Fanny Keats before he formally called upon her at her guardian's.

2 Wm. Ewing, sculptor, is frequently mentioned in Severn's letters. He be-friended Keats and Severn in the painful days preceding the former's death, was present at his burial, and assisted Severn in his difficulties with the Italian health authorities. Early in May, 1821, Ewing returned to England, bringing with him a letter of introduction to Charles Brown who, he records, 'received me very kindly.'

Thursday evening
[November 15, 1821.]

    I have been waiting, My dear Fanny, some time in the expectation of hearing you were arrived in London for the winter, affraid to write lest the letter should be too late and without any means of ascertaining the truth as my brother [1] *was in the country and I do not know any one else in the habit of going to the city. As soon as he returned I sent him with a note for you and heard to my great surprize you were not expected for a week. When you do come I shall be very glad to see you directly you find it convenient—I hope by that time you will have had an opportunity of reading some of your books—I don't at all think you will succeed in making M*rs *Abby a literary lady—I go on as usual, reading every trumpery novel that comes in my way spoiling my taste and understanding, as for acquaintance I see none unless I take the trouble of going after them. M*r *Guiterez must needs call one day when there was no one at home so I know nothing of him —I have been a few days at M*rs *Dilkes there I heard only one thing to please me, she has quarrelled, I hope for* ever with the Reynolds. My dear Fanny if you live [to] the age of the Methuselem and I die tomorrow never be intimate with the Reynolds,[2] for I dare say they will come your way—Mrs Dilke cannot keep up a feud and perhaps will be friends again. Every day I live I find out more of their malice against me—I don't know whether you wish particularly to see Mrs Dilke but I shall I think bring her yet. I like so much more to be with you by myself—

     I wish I knew what books you have read for I would write about them, there is nothing I like better to talk about unless it is to such a very great judge that I am affraid they will think all my delightful criticism nonsense. So I hope you are not one of these terrible persons or will not let me know it for depend on it I should neither open my lips or move my pen on the subject and so you would lose the benefit of my opinion—I must also beg you will not learn whole verses or chapters &c to dodge me for though I can remember pretty well generally I read too many things to do so particularly—so what you may take for a proof of stupidity, is on the contrary through the great extensiveness of my studies.

     I was almost affraid of sending my brother to enquire after you, for he has got a white coat and I am afraid

fancies himself a man so it would have looked suspicious,
particularly if he had left the note

  Hoping to see you soon, I remain, my dearest Fanny,
    Yours most affectionately

            F. Brawne

POSTMARK: Hampstead 12 o'clock, Nov. 16. 1821. ni. Ev.
ADDRESS: *For Miss Keats*
    Richard Abbeys Esq
    Walthamstow.

1 Samuel Brawne, then 17. He died at Wentworth Place, at the age of 23, in 1828.
2 In *Papers of a Critic*, Sir C.W. Dilke, Bt., writes (Memoir of C.W. Dilke): 'Miss Reynolds writes to Mrs. Dilke, "I hear that Keats is going to Rome, which must please all his friends on every account. I sincerely hope it will benefit his health. Poor fellow! His mind and spirits must be bettered by it; and absence may probably weaken, if not break off, a connection that has been a most unhappy one for him." '

Monday night.
[Between November 17th and December 12th, 1821.]

My dear Fanny

I have asked Mr. Brown to look for your age.[1]
Alas it is not there but if you will let me know where you
were christened, if it be in London, my brother will get
your register a day or so after I receive your letter—He
has been getting one for my aunt and knows the way—I
have no pity whatever for your nerves because I have no
nerves, but I think your dislike to the word criticism quite
proper, it is a very ugly foolish word—and heaven forbid
we should ever use it—you may rate your powers that way
as low as you please but as I consider mine only worth
three halfpence I dare say you won't think them lower than
that—Don't suppose I ever open my lips about books be-
fore men at all clever and stupid men I treat too ill to
talk to at all. Women generally talk of very different
things—Don't you or do you admire Don Juan? perhaps
you like the serious parts best but I have been credibly in-
formed that Lord B. is not really *a great poet,*[2] *have taken*

*a sort of dislike to him when serious and only adore him
for his wit and humour. I am by no means a great poetry
reader—and like few things not comic out of Shakespeare.
Comedy of all sorts pleases me. I think Beppo nearly as
good as Don Juan. When you read it you will notice
that gratifying account of us English young ladies—I believe I did not tell you that Donna Inez was intended for
Lady Byron to whom he wrote that fine sentimental, 'Fare
thee well.' The character is beautiful and I have no doubt
very like for I have heard Lady B. is a bluestocking. One
thing is certain to me, which is, that it is impossible to
write about books, for before you can get out your sensations about one line the letter is finished—but it is always
better to talk about them—Llanos was here the other day
looking bad enough and more like a Frenchman than a
Spaniard—I keep that name for best, and in common call
him Guiterez—*

*I who call on nobody have actually four calls and
two visits to make as soon as the weather will suffer it,
besides yours which is a visitation, in M^{rs} A's opinion at
any rate. I do believe I always stay 3 hours and I should
like to stay six—Don't suppose that is a bit of a compli-
ment stuck in at the end of a letter for I never can make
compliments which is no merit but a great awkwardness*

and particularly foolish in me who am not at all bashfull and hardly modest—I shall send this at a venture to London —If the day you appoint is very wet I will put it off to the next and so on—Good night. I have got all my hair to curl, everybody is in bed and the fire half out—I shall put up prayers tonight that you may be able to make out most of this letter.

Yours very affectionately

F B

NO ADDRESS OR POSTMARK.

1 Fanny Keats was 18½. See Letter No. 11. 'Mr. Brown . . . has a large bible.'
2 A reflection of Keats's opinion of Lord Byron.

Thursday Dec. 13th
[1821.]

My dear Fanny

before I began to write I thought I had a great deal to say to you and now I cannot recollect a word of any thing of consequence. You will find by the register I enclose that you are but 18, for which I am very sorry but the register will always be of use particularly when you are of age to show Mr Abbey as without so good an evidence he might doubt your word—I like Mrs Abbey's attempts the other day to make you but seventeen—a worthless old woman. You will see that I have not forgotten the story she told me—I saw Mrs Henderson yesterday but quite forgot to ask her about it—I dined with Mrs Dilke a day or two after I saw you. She asked whether you were in town but luckily never inquired whether I had seen you yet so I equivocated which you know is much the same as telling a story at once and said I did not mean to call on you at present for fear the Abbey's should think I came too often, true enough.

We dine with them on Christmas day which is like

54

most people's Christmas day's melancholy enough. What must yours be? I ask that question in no exultation. I cannot think it will be much worse than mine for I have to remember that three years ago was the happiest day I had ever then spent,[1] but I will not touch on such subjects for there are much better times and ways to remember them—I think you will like the great part of the Indicator I sent you—there are two pieces of poetry in it signed Caviare, by your brother.[2] I never open it for he is connected with every page—

Tuesday Dec[br] 18th. When I had written so far I was called away and have never been able to finish till today—I was at a party last night the first real party I have been to this year—You would have laughed had you seen me dressed out in my cap &c—I did feel a little queer —I have not written to Mr. Wylie[3] nor am I sure that I shall ever summon courage to do so—But you have no right to blame me for a little modesty, so dont feel disappointed if you never get the picture at all—To be sure it is very dishonest of him to keep it—I shall if I can find it, enclose you M[rs] George's hair—and then you will not be able to accuse me of anything of the sort.

I remain my dear Fanny

Yours most affectionately F.B.

Finding it is impossible which coloured hair I liked best of the two curls tied together, and once flourishing on my fair head, I have sent both—they will serve to show you the mutability of all human things—though as different as possible they were cut off within a year of each other— how my hair must have changed [4] for the better or worse— The oddest thing is the dark one was cut off first.

POSTMARK: Hampstead, 12 o'clock, De. 19. 1821. NN.
ADDRESS: *For Miss Keats*
         No. 4 Pancras Lane
            Cheapside—

1 The day on which she probably became engaged to John Keats.
2 The *Indicator*, the number of May 10th, 1820, contained 'La Belle Dame sans Mercy,' that of June 28th, the sonnet 'As Hermes once,' both signed 'Caviare.' Both printed for the first time.
3 Henry or Charles Wylie, brothers-in-law of George Keats.
4 Amy Lowell, vol. ii, p. 135, writes: 'She was prostrated and seriously ill for some time.' There is no mention of illness in these letters, but the comment on the change in colour of her hair is curious.

Sunday Evening
[February 3rd 1822.]

My Dear Fanny

    I forgot the last time I saw you to ask whether you could spare me the two London Magazines with the English Opium Eater in.[1] *I do not want them for myself, but M*r *Brown, awkward enough, came for them the very day I sent them to you; as it was of no immediate consequence, I would not unpack them, particularly as I thought he might as well get them from the library, a day or two ago he mentioned them again, so, if you* have read them I will *send the carrier any day you like, but do not hurry, he only wants to consult something in them, which I have no doubt will be in as good time a month hence.* The next *time I come to see you I will be earlier whether M*rs *Dilke is with me or not—that is what makes me dislike bringing her she likes me to set out from her house and I know she cannot be ready in time.* I *am very bad, but* I *can get ready on some occasions for instance, whenever I have come to see you it has been generally early enough.* A few nights *after, my brother and I went to the play with her and when we got there the first act was nearly over; exactly this time twelvemonth we went with her to the same place and just at the same time. To the end of all this I must however tack a little confession, that except Mrs Dilke I am the worst person in the world for being ready—*

You are a naughty girl for what little of your books you can read you never tell me a word about. I hope you will not, from my asking for the two books, hurry with the rest for you are perfectly welcome to them for years, which is saying nothing for nobody returns a Pamphlet or newspaper—under nine months.

How I liked that sly question about Mr Guiterez that morning. I did not dare look up for fear of laughing but it amused me to see how people commit themselves by trying to see through others. I felt so glad I had told you because I thought it must have delighted you as it did me. It was quite a scene—How very delightful it would be to have you with me tonight, I am quite alone. I am always glad to get my 'family' out (to provoke me they scarcely ever go) and then highly favored indeed is the person I would wish for or even admit. There is one and only one person in the world besides yourself that I would admit tonight and her coming is about as possible as yours. So *you see you are highly favored—I was asked out to tea by some friends who thought I must feel 'lonely'—for my part I think people are all mad—*

Tomorrow night I am going to the play and I think you will own I like it by the trouble I take, for I am obliged to walk to town, meet my brother, and walk home with him at night, because at certain parts of the year (that is, a month or two after quarter day) we can neither of us afford to ride—

I remain my dear Fanny's

Very affectionate Frances Brawne—

POSTMARK: 7 o'clock, Feb. 4. 1822. Aft.
ADDRESS: *For Miss Keats*
　　　No. 4 Pancras Lane,
　　　　Cheapside.

1 First published in the *London Magazine*, October and November, 1821.

My dear Fanny

  Though it is not above a month since I saw you the time seems unusually long. In a day or two I am going out for a few days and when I return I shall be so much engaged that I shall not call in Pancras lane for some weeks; which I do not regret for I dare say Mrs Abby makes herself more disagreeable than usual whenever you have any of your friends to see you. What an uncomfortable way we are obliged to see each other in. Two years ¹ seems a long while to look forward, yet I do look forward to the end of that time and think with the greatest pleasure how different our acquaintance (I don't like the word friendship) will be then, at least I hope so, and I am sure if you feel as well disposed towards it as I do, we shall be very happy together. One thing you can do, which is, to let me know if you go to any public places, exhibitions &c. There I should feel more at my ease with you than in any house belonging to Mr Abbey—If you write to me you had

better direct as usual; my Mother will forward the letters.
One of the places I am going to is Hampton Court.   I
would give the world if you could go with me the palace
is so beautiful, at least I think so, who never saw any
other.   If you see anything you like particularly in the books
mind you mention it

>   *I remain yours affectionately*
>   *My dear Fanny*
>   *Frances Brawne*

Postmark: Hampstead, 12 o'clock, Mr. 18. 1822. M.
Address: *Miss Keats*
>   *at Mr. Abbeys*
>   *No. 4 Pancras Lane*
>   *Cheapside.*

1 Fanny Keats would be 21 on June 3rd, 1824.

Hampstead—May 7th
[1822.]

My dearest Fanny

If you thought me bad before what must you consider me now—I am affraid past all forgiveness but when
you hear that I only returned last night and then saw your
letter for the first time, I hope you will own that I am not
quite so bad.

The truth is that instead of staying a fortnight at
Hampton I stayed nearly five weeks and then I was with
Mrs Dilke a day or two before I went home. My Mother
did not forward the letter because she did not know where
I was and expected me every day, after the first three weeks.
I had two reasons for not writing to you, one was that I
never write to any one when I am from home and the other
that having no idea of staying so long I intended whenever
I did write to fix a day for calling on you, for I never
thought of your leaving town yet—how very little I have
seen of you this winter and yet I have only missed one op-
portunity, which was just before I left home—now I think of
it perhaps we shall meet at the exhibition I am going there

with Mrs Dilke in about ten days, but if,—when you go, you can give me a tolerable long notice, I think I can meet you there.

Your pigeons, my dear girl, I accept with the greatest pleasure, they come at a very good time, when I have just lost my favorite cat. You must give me directions how to keep them and whether I am to get them a house. I hope they will stay with me—If a boy can bring them I will send to Walthamstow, if you like. You must tell me if they are to be kept indoors or out—We have no outhouses nothing but a tool house—Will they, if let out, join other pigeons and leave me? I ask these questions because I should be sorry to lose them through my inexperience. I mean to read what Buffon[1] says of pigeons, tonight.

I have read Buffon but he gives me no account how I am to feed them, so I must rely entirely on you. The very first time Mrs Abbey comes to town I will certainly call on you—in a week's time I shall be staying with Mrs Dilke but I shall leave orders for all letters to be sent directly; though I have no doubt I shall hear from you before I go— If I happen to be staying there at the time you come to town I shall bring her with me, if I am at home I shall come by myself—which I should prefer.—

Oh Fanny I wish to goodness you were two or three years older—I get quite disheartened when I think of it—

I suppose you have seen by this time that Byron was very little concerned in the affair you mentioned, and that his being arrested is a mistake[2]*—I have been very comfortable and* [for *at*] *Hampton. There is a palace there built by Cardinal Wolsey, a great part of it filled with pictures, I went over it several times and made a vow to myself—that as soon as you were free from your present slavery I would take you down to see it—M*ʳ *Guiterez' brother is gone to join the independents in South America rather odd that, to fight against his own country*[3]*—*

God bless you, dear Fanny

Yours most affectionately   *F B—*

POSTMARK: Hampstead, 8 o'clock, My. 8. 1822. Ev. & NI.
ADDRESS: *For Miss Keats*
    Richard Abbey's Esq.
    Walthamstow.

1 Comte de Buffon (1707–88). Published his *Natural History*, 1749–67.
2 This probably alludes to the fracas between Lord Byron, Count Gamba, Captain Hay, Shelley and Trelawny, and the Italian hussar, who on passing them on horseback violently jostled one of the party; Byron overtook him and there was a violent quarrel, following which the Englishmen were threatened with arrest. Blows were exchanged and Italian soldiers were wounded. Byron's servants were arrested, and ultimately banished, and with them the Counts Gamba, father and son. See Medwin's *Conversations with Lord Byron*, 1824, p. 375.
3 The struggle for independence in Brazil. On Oct. 12th, 1822, relations with Portugal were severed, and Dom Pedro was made constitutional Emperor. War followed, and the Portuguese fleet was defeated by Lord Cochrane, commanding the Brazilian navy.

My dear Fanny

I am a bad person to refer to, because you know my extravagance, but I really think over economy the most expensive thing there is, if you have a body to your grey silk you cannot get it made under a guinea or perhaps 25 shillings and it will be of very little use to you afterwards as short sleeves &c are not much worn out of full dress particularly to you who are not much in the habit of seeing company, not that I would advise you to have a new dress if you cannot get it for 30 shillings but I suppose you might have a clear muslin for that money, I mention clear muslin because a silk petticoat would not be necessary, as I know many who wear them without, and I dont think there is any difference in the appearance, gowns are made quite plain so that there is very little expense as to trimming. I have seen some made in crepe lisse that would do very well for a pattern for muslin; with two folds of the same stuff as the gown, one straight round the bottom, forming the hem, the other brought to a point in front (on one side) and finished with a flower, in this manner.—

If you should have it be sure to let them put no colours about the gown, nothing but white, indeed I do not like any sattin at all, the bands of course will be put in with small cords covered with muslin: as to the body I saw one the other day at Mrs Morgans made for a dance quite plain as to trimming something like the make of my red and black, but lower round *the* throat *and confined at the shoulders in three bands so as to let the fulness go over the shoulders as well as in the front. The back something the same, but very little fulness except at the bottom of the waist. The sleeve as you see is a plain one of the usual size, with a frill round the arm, which you can put in lace:*

this pattern will I think do for the grey body, if you find the muslin makes a great difference in the expence for then it certainly would be better to have the grey. I should be sorry to persuade you to any extra expence, but you buy your things yourself and can therefore get them very reasonable and I believe they do not charge you a great deal for making them, you must not have a very coarse muslin. Still, if you are not likely to go to any more parties I really would have the grey. I think net sleeves out of the question. I believe this is all I can say on the subject—and now for a favor from you. Do if you have a hen pigeon to spare let me have it, but I would rather go without unless you can be certain it is a hen. Perhaps you may have one that is a widow—by cats &c. I dare not trust to one about which you are not certain for I have no room as it is, and Mary & Trutken are obliged to lodge in another house.

The cats have taken Primrose, and I would not have any more but I have so many that have no wives. Do not hurry about [it] but when you go to Walthamstow if you can find one to suit me, let me know. I owe you a brown-wings, but I have had no young ones yet though Trutken

*has be[en] setting for some time, but as he is a young be-
ginner I suppose he will spoil the first pair or two.*

Yours truly,

Frances Brawne

POSTMARK TORN.

ADDRESS: *For Miss Keats,*
4, *Pancras Lane,*
Queen Street,
Cheapside.

[Summer, 1822.]

My dear Fanny

I left Hampton last thursday summoned to town by a letter from Margaret [1] *to the following effect.* 'Dear Fanny, for heaven's sake come home directly, Mr Romay* [2] *leaves Hampstead on the* 8th *for Brussels'—This was nearly the whole of her letter and you may conceive the effect, every day seemed an age untill I could set to town.* *Alas, it is too true that he leaves Hampstead next sunday, but there is a chance of their going to Guernsey instead of Brussels and I do not think they will leave London immediately, but did you ever know any thing more wretched?* *Our hopes of comfort are at an end.* *You may take your leave of the guitar.* *When you write me I shall expect to hear that you are in despair.* *I will send the gown to Pancras Lane tomorrow but I am affraid you will find a high gown of little use especially as I guess by the blouse it will be rather a dress one, remember if you go to any dances next winter you will want a gown low to the neck, and from being thin you would look a thousand times better in white* *silk or muslin. If however you still intend to have a gown à la Jacke, there is a french sleeve worn that would be very becoming to you. The top sleeve I send you is 6 fingers and ½ wide. The sleeve I want to describe has the same sort of top but about eleven fingers wide and falls below the elbow where it is joined in with straps so as to set close to the arm. I will try to draw it, but it can be only to make you understand, not your dressmaker.*

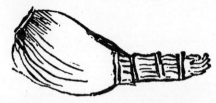

What I have drawn is, God knows, as unlike a sleeve with an arm in it, as heart can wish, and gives no great idea of my skill in drawing; the fine strokes at the top are the gathers which are set in fine plaits, and the pieces between the straps are separate and of a equal size, it takes a great deal of silk, I dare say and you may not like the idea so do not be over persuaded *to have it— if you have a double cape, which I think you ought with blouse it takes two yards and a half but I am not sure that fringe will not look richer unless it is to be full dress.—I spent a tolerably pleasant 3 weeks at Hampton, I went to Windsor, which was the best part of it, I did not go to*

Hampton Court, as I know it very well, besides which, I told my Aunt I should like to take you to see it, so that any Saturday in the autumn that you will like to go with me she will be very glad to see you, only be sure to give me a weeks notice, but there will be time enough to talk of that. I shall send this letter to Walthamstow that you may know the gown is in town. Margaret and I are red hot to make a chinks gown apiece. Mine is to be à la Jacke; a pattern she is unfortunately barred from, in consequence of the obstinate imitations of the 3 Miss Richardsons.

   If I write any more you will not get your letter today so

   I remain my dear Fanny
   Yours affectionately

   Frances Brawne

   I shall send the gown this morning.
   Finished Monday Morning.
   My Mother sends her love, and is extremely obliged to you for the melon which is a very fine one. Give our

Comp^ts and thanks to Mr Abbey and remember me to Miss A—.

DELIVERED BY HAND.
ADDRESS: *Miss Keats*
        Richard Abbeys Esq.
        Walthamstow.

1 Margaret was Fanny's younger sister.
2 Mr. Romay: perhaps a teacher of music and dancing.

Friday.
[Summer, 1822.]

My dear Fanny

    I really am so teized by different things I scarcely know what I am doing. I have destroyed your letter forgetting you wanted an answer about your pelisse. I would have written yesterday but thinking I remembered you were to be in town tomorrow I wanted to ask you to come here tomorrow night, and I would if I could, go to town with you Monday morning. This I am prevented from doing as my Aunt is staying here and should she remain I should not be able to give you a bed; but she may be gone and at all events I will send a note to you in Pancras Lane by the carrier tomorrow, if you are in town I hope you will come if I am able to say in it that she is gone. She talks of doing so, most positively, but my Mother may persuade her to alter her mind—I shall send this to Walthamstow though in the greatest uncertainty whether you may not be in town, so in the letter to town tomorrow I shall repeat all I have said now.—The reason I want you to come is that the

Romay's leave town next wednesday, and they may come out on sunday, though I know nothing about it as I am now expecting them, but in consequence of a horrible train of mistakes which have nearly driven me mad, I am much affraid they will not come—You must come if my Aunt is gone. The Abbeys cannot think it strange of your coming for so short a time if however I am prevented from seeing you the best dressmaker I know is Mrs Bell, 62 Newman Street—Oxford Street—She is not very expeditious but as she cannot have much to do at this time of the year, if you fix your time she may let you have it soon enough—if you prefer Mrs Morgan, her direction is 37, St. James' Place, St. James' Street—but she is very expensive, you had better know the price in either case and I think it would be as well to mention my name.—

Yours very affectionately

Frances Brawne

My Mother thinks my Aunt will stay plague take it but I shall write again—

Saturday Morn
[August, 1822.]

My dear Fanny

    I met Mr Wylie a short time ago, and he told me he believed his brother had called on you.—If he did so, on the day he intended I think it would have been about four days after you left London—I asked him where you could send your letter he did not tell me his brother's direction but said you had better enclose it to him, at No. 11 Union Terrace Camden town. The postman did not cheat you about the papers, I find they must be put in at Lombard Street to go free, and then I am not sure that they may not charge a penny for each—Let me know if they do so. I shall miss one week's paper as it is not a very proper one —I want to send you a magazine and a volume of Shakespeare, how shall I get them to you? I am affraid my pigeons will soon be building another nest—I find it will not be possible to get them out of the present one I must wait till they choose to bring the young ones, but as they are said to lay every month and it is three weeks since they began to set I am affraid the hen will have eggs in another week or ten days particularly as some people tell me they appear to be building in a fresh place. A book that I have read says 'should the cock or hen be lost when they have young, the remaining parent will bring them up,' and it also says that, 'soon after the young come out of the shell the hen leaves them to the cock and lays again.' Should you think it would be safe for me to confine the hen by herself? I shall do nothing till I hear from you which I hope to do, the beginning of the week—It is very easy to catch them. I am so fearful of losing the post that I will leave off here

Yours affectionately my dear Girl

Frances Brawne

POSTMARK IMPERFECT: Au. 1822. N.
ADDRESS: *For Miss Keats*
   Richard Abbey's Esq.
   Walthamstow.

Tuesday Morning
[October 15, 1822.]

My dear Fanny

    I should have written to you some time ago but I have had a bad hand from a gentle bite given me by my dog,[1] *even now I am not sure you will be able to read what I have written for my hand is so tied up that I can scarcely make use of the pen, however you must try—I am quite in despair about my pigeons, I believe they are the most refractory pair in the kingdom—they never lay more than one egg and never make anything of that—After the one I told you they had quarrelled with, they had another which they broke immediately,—again about a week back they laid one which untill last night they sat on with great care, but this morning it was found pushed out of the nest like the first and cracked so awkwardly had they performed the operation. I mention its being cracked because that might be the reason they would not hatch it —It is supposed they must have had a matrimonial quarrel in the middle of the night for a great scream was heard at*

*that time by my Mother from one of them after which all
was quiet—Now in applying to you to know whether you
can account for it I consider I am taking counsel's opinion
on the subject so pray give it with all due gravity—I must
just add that I am pretty certain no one had in any way
touched or molested them—in consequence of my hand I
have [not] fed them [myself] this fortnight or more, but
the housemaid who has done them for me, is by no means
a person to touch forbidden things particularly as she knew
the consequences—and we only knew they had an egg by
their constantly setting,—so much for them. I will try
them in confinement a little longer, after that if they do
no better they shall be left to themselves—Mrs Dilke is returned and next time I call to see you I shall bring her
if I know of it in time. Mr Brown is safely arrived at
Pisa and in spite of his vow has made an acquaintance
with Lord Byron, he liked him very much²—I have been
reading Gil Blas³ again and I like it as well as ever, but
I do not wonder at your disappointment for it is so totally
different from Don Quixote and wants the romantic parts
so much besides showing so much of the worst part of the
world that to many people it must be a very disagreable*

book—I remember hating it at first—I will not write any
longer for fear of straining my hand
Yours very affectionately

Frances Brawne

POSTMARK: 12 o'clock, Oc. 15. 1822.
ADDRESS: *For Miss Keats,*
Richard Abbeys Esq.
Walthamstow.

1 'Carlo, Mrs. Brawne's dog.' (*Letters*, p. 459.)

2 Brown arrived at Pisa on Aug. 31st, 1822, where he met Byron and Trelawny. In an unpublished letter from Severn to his father, Dec. 7th, 1822, Severn writes: 'Then I meet my friend Mr. Brown in Florence, who is to introduce me to Lord Byron.' In a later letter to his sister he mentions that Lord Byron and Trelawny are preparing to go to Greece, and defends them against their bad reputation in England.

3 By A. R. Le Sage.

Undated. [October 29, 1822.]

My dear Fanny

I intended to have called in the city for three days last week but was prevented each time: twice by company and once by the weather, so that I shall call some day next week and take the chance of seeing you. Not that I much expect you to be there, but as I shall be going to see a friend it will not be out of my way. Thank you for your enquiries about my hand, it would not have been so bad but the dog was ill at the time he did it and the doctor thought it better to provide against the consequences that always may *follow a dog's bite. Carlo was not the least in the wrong it was entirely my fault, he, poor fellow is since dead from something he had swallowed, but I shall have quite a long story to tell you about it when we meet. —I shall certainly take your advice about the pigeons, but at present I am waiting till they lay again, which will make things safer, and which I expect them to do very soon, they generally set on the egg a few days before they have the misfortune to break it which accident, I really be-*

lieve happens from their fondness for it, as both wish to hatch at once; it is people of this disposition that invariably spoil their children and bring them up such plagues as no doubt I was, and for what I know may be still. There is, I think, every prospect of a reconciliation between M*rs* Dilke and the Reynolds', for M*r* J. Reynolds is married,[1] the Dilkes have called on him and have been informed that his sisters are very anxious to make up the quarrel, fine fun it will be to see them together. I shall send you the papers up to last sunday but that of today is at present lent to a friend and I would not wait any longer before I wrote—I always send the papers and a letter together as I fancy the postman's visits might occasion suspicion if too often repeated—I hope I do not miss any, but I am sure to forget the date of the last you had: I also hope you do not pay anything now—

I remain, My dear Fanny
Yours affectionately

Frances Brawne

I see I have mentioned in the beginning of my note that it is owing to the doctor my hand was so bad; but as I have *not told you what was done, perhaps you will fancy, as my cousins did, that a terrible operation was performed, my hand dissected and half-carried away and a most delightfully horrible story it was, but unfortunately for those who delight in these wonders I had only a little caustic applied, which is nothing at all to talk about—*

POSTMARK: Fenchurch St. 4 o'clock, Oc. 29. 1822. Ev.
ADDRESS: *For Miss Keats*
> *Richard Abbey's Esq.*
> *Walthamstow.*

1 John Hamilton Reynolds married Miss Eliza Powell Drewe Aug. 31st, 1822.

Undated. [1823.]

My dear Fanny

Upon looking at my Shakespeare [1] *I find it so very large that you would not be able, without great inconvenience to take it home with you particularly with the addition of other books.—I have therefore sent you Spencer* [2] *instead, which you will feel the more pleasure in reading as you will find the best parts marked by one who I have heard called the best judge of poetry living—they were marked for me to read and I need not tell you with what pleasure I did so. Keep them as long as you wish for I never open them now. The serious poems of Lord Byron were given me by a schoolfellow; who was once my great friend but as this friendship has gone off into a mere acquaintance I do not feel bound to keep [them] for her sake you are therefore wellcome to them if you think them worth keeping. I can remember being half wild about them learning and repeating continually when alone but as my dear Keats did not admire Lord Byrons poetry as many people do, it soon lost its value with me. If I am not mistaken he thought Manfred one of the best—*

84

Of the rest Beppo is now known to be his; I send the Vampire [3] *which has nothing particular to recommend it, but being at first published as Lord B——'s, who however did not write it—Beppo and the first Don Juan are considered by* all *very clever. The second volume of Don Juan you will not I think like so well—I shall be glad to hear how you like the different books—I send but one magazine on account of the size but you mentioned having so little prose that I thought it might not be unpleasant—The review on Endymion is written by a Mr Patmore,* [4] *who was much talked of some time ago through a duel he was second in. You I dare say know that the Mr Scott killed was the editor of this very magazine* [5]*—If I do not find the parcel too large I will put in the second magazine* [6] *because you will find in it all that occasioned the duel— The articles called table talk are very good—they are by Mr Hazlitt—those signed Elia are considered very beautiful —Charles Lamb is the name of the author. In this I give your dear brother's opinion as far as I could get it now* [7] *—all these books are of no consequence to me and I read only the most amusing.—Any of them you already have it will be better to pack up and leave in town, then let me know by a letter and I will send my carrier who is as good as a footman—The Shakespeare I will send when you are*

in town for the winter, it will then amuse you and there
will be no trouble in carrying it about—When you write
will you tell me what you know of your brother George,
yesterday I forgot to ask.[8]*—Mrs Dilke is anxious to know*
where he is, as Mr William Dilke[9] *would like to write to*
him—I went to westminster after I left you yesterday and
tomorrow I go there again.   Mrs Dilke desired her best
love and was very much disappointed she had not seen you.

Now I must, like the country people beg pardon for
all mistakes but I have written in such a hurry, expecting
the carrier every minute, that I hardly know what I am
about as you will see—I remain my dearest girl

Yours most affectionately

F. Brawne

No Postmark.
Address: *Miss Keats.*

---

1 This was the facsimile of the First Folio of Shakespeare's Works, given by Keats to Fanny Brawne before he left for Italy.   Now in the Keats Museum.
2 Keats writes to Fanny Brawne, May, 1820: 'I have been employed in marking the most beautiful passages in Spenser, intending it for you.'   The book was lost in Germany.
3 *The Vampire, a tale*, by John Wm. Polidori.   1819.   London.
4 Peter George Patmore (1786–1855), father of Coventry Patmore.
5 John Scott and J. H. Christie fought a duel following Scott's denouncement of 'Z' in the *London Magazine*.   Lockhart challenged Scott, but his friend Christie took his place.   Scott was mortally wounded and died six weeks later.   The *London Magazine* for March, 1821, states in 'The Lion's Head' that the meeting took place 'between Mr. Scott and the friend of Mr. Lockhart's on Friday,

February the 16th, and it was hoped that the imminent danger which attended the wound had subsided.' 'The Lion's Head' is dated Feb. 26th, 1821. Fanny Brawne took some interest in the Scott-Christie duel, for Brown writing to Thomas Richards on Feb. 18th, 1821, says: 'Miss Brawne has just told me she has heard that the ball has been extracted, and that Scott is likely to recover.'

6 The *London Magazine*. Fanny Brawne was evidently sending bound volumes, not monthly parts. See next letter.

7 Keats records his admiration of Hazlitt; that he admired Charles Lamb also is new.

8 George Keats had settled at Louisville, Kentucky, U.S.A.

9 C. W. Dilke's brother, who had built a house on an adjoining plot of land, naming it Wentworth House.

[Monday, July 28, 1823.]

My dear Fanny

You are usually so punctual a correspondent that I am quite surprised I have not heard from you in answer to my note from Hampton. Not that it is of any consequence for I left Mrs Dilke last wednesday, three or four days sooner than I expected in consequence of Mr W. Dilke's being expected in London, for fear there should be any mistake between your town and country house I shall get my brother to enquire in Pancras lane, for your present residence. I have been from home so much during the last three or four months that I am quite bewildered as to the dates of the last magazines &c. you have received. I which [for wish] you would write me word whether you would like all the papers you have missed and what the last was you received. If you have finished Spencer or any of the bound magazines I will send you some more. I have so few books that I cannot lend you all I wish you to read, as I am obliged to get them from the library, but the other volumes of Shakespeare you can have when ever

you like—I passed a pleasant time at Hampton and saw
my old favorite Hampton Court several times. I hope to
take you there yet, only a twelvemonth,[1] Fanny, from last
June. You had better begin Mrs Abbey's veil soon or she
will never have it, bye the bye I have learnt some stitches
for that sort of work and if you like I will show them
to you. I hope to see you soon,

and remain, yours very affectionately

Frances Brawne

Monday—

POSTMARK: Lombard St. Ev. Jy. 29. 1823.
ADDRESS: *For Miss Keats*
Richard Abbey's Esq.
Walthamstow.

1 Referring to Fanny Keats's coming of age on June 3rd, 1824.

[November 16, 1823.]

My dear Fanny

Heaven knows how you have gone on with the allum baskets but I am annoyed to death—I sent to a lady to know the quantity of logwood [1] *I ought to put and her answer was that she had never in her life mentioned logwood to me but that cochineal would have the same effect. I had not time then to write to you and instead of returning home in a few days as I expected I stayed out a fortnight; since I came home I have tried two baskets and could not make either of them do well. The cochineal instead of turning to lilac makes a faint pink which is very pretty—I powdered it first very fine put some boiling water on it and poured it into a saucepan when nearly cold. To a gallon and a half of water I put as much cochineal as came to a penny. After I wrote to you I saw a basket at Mrs Dilkes which I admired so much that it induced me to try my luck, instead of being crossed, it was entirely covered with allum and very faintly coloured with the logwood, if you still wish to try logwood with yours you had better mix certain* quantities together and see how it looks when dry—But no doubt I shall see you soon and can tell you more about it —I met the Lancasters at a quadrille party at the Davenports[2]—I think Miss Lancaster plain and very common and ungenteel looking. Mr Guiterez was there, the beau of the room[3]—He has been here this morning and I expect him again tonight—Would you believe it I quarrelled with him but I hope it is now made up—for the defence of my character, I must mention that he was quite in the wrong— I don't know whether I mentioned that Miss Rowcroft is going to South America immediately

I remain my dear Girl

Yours very affectionately

Frances Brawne

Sunday evening

POSTMARK: Nov. 17, 1823.
ADDRESS: *For Miss Keats*
        Richard Abbey's Esq.
        Walthamstow.

1 A vegetable dyestuff used for fabrics.
2 Burridge Davenport lived in Church Row, Hampstead. Keats frequently visited Mr. and Mrs. Davenport when living at Wentworth Place. There is an unpublished letter in the British Museum, dated November, 1818, from Keats to Mrs. Davenport thanking her for her inquiries about Tom's health.
3 It is evident that by this date Llanos was well acquainted with the friends of the Brawnes in Hampstead.

Friday.
[February 27, 1824.]

My dear Fanny

If I do not write to you tonight I shall not send you a letter for two or three weeks as I am very busy at present with some work I want finished at the beginning of next week. Miss Rowcroft is very ill, confined to her bed with inflammation of the lungs but I do not expect them to go for two or three weeks—Don't alarm yourself about Miss Lancasters appearance, I trust you would cut a better figure than she did. You might feel shy at first (which is not that I know of her failing) but any person of sense who goes out a little can soon get over all that—dress, manner and carriage are just what she wants, a person must be a great beauty to look well without them, but they are certainly within the reach of any body of understanding— perhaps Miss L. might look particularly bad that night. Don't suppose it was a grand party there could not be above forty people and their rooms are small, but it was a very pleasant one—we are going there next week, only to a card

party a piece of the entertainment I could dispense with—
Margaret Davenport [1] is rather a genteel girl and I think
I told you the second sister is very pretty—Lancaster is
likely to be at our house tomorrow night but I don't know
that I shall be at home—The only place to get the baskets
that I can find is the bazaar dont you think Mrs Abbey
will let you walk there with me? I will be with you by
ten o'clock and we may be back in time for your dinner
for I suppose it impossible to get off from the unconscionable
hour of half past two—Did I ever think to hear of people
dining at such a time in a christian country—I have got
a new pigeon a husband for one of my single ladies but
the other is such a beauty (they call her a dragon pouter)
that I shall wait till I can marry her more to my satisfaction—The newcomer is a dragon runt—Miss Rowcroft is
not in the city but if she returns there and I go to see her
I shall call on you, whether I have heard from you or not
—My Mother was in Pancras Lane the other day to enquire after your health for you had not written for some
time and I was affraid you were ill, she saw the coachman
and sent her compliments which I think it probable he kept
for his own benefit—It will ever remain a mystery to me
whether it is possible to read a letter written in this greasy
ink, I have all but sworn at it—If you will have read the

single *magazines* especially *those with the Spanish poetry, by the time I see you I will, if you please, bring them away as I am asked to lend them to a gentleman—With compliments to M*rs* *and Miss Abbey I remain*

yours very affectionately

F B—

*Let me know whether M*rs* *A. is likely to let you take a walk with me that I may be with you early—I shall be obliged to go and see Miss Rowcroft tomorrow but she is not near you even were you in town—* F B

POSTMARK: Hampstead. 27 Feb. 24. Night.
ADDRESS: *Miss Keats*
Richard Abbeys Esq.
Walthamstow.

1 Daughter of Burridge Davenport. See note above.

[June 2, 1824.]

My dear Fanny

Your letter has quite shocked me, can it indeed be four months since I wrote to you? I am certain you must possess the most forgiving disposition in the world to write to me after such neglect. Except that I ought to be and generally am, more careful in remembering you, than any one else, I could assure you that you are by no means the only person towards whom I deserve to be ashamed of my behaviour. Miss Rowcroft's brother, came here a few weeks ago, entirely to give me news of her and to beg of me to write to her immediately which I have not yet done; as to Mʳˢ Dilke I believe she is quite affronted with me. Don't suppose that I should not have shame enough to keep these things, only you seem to suspect that while I neglect you I may be more attentive elsewhere, this is so far from the case, that you have been untill very lately the only person excepted from my general inattention. Lancaster was at our house last wednesday and promised to call here on sunday for some books for you, but I suppose he forgot it as I

have never seen him, so I shall bring them on thursday.
I have not forgotten that the 18th of June is your birthday.[1]
I am invited to a party for that night.

    I must now conclude as I wish the letter to go by
this post and the clock has struck

            Yours very affectionately

                      F B

I will see you thursday

POSTMARK: Hampstead, June 2nd. 1824.
ADDRESS: *Miss Keats*
4 *Pancras Lane*
Cheapside

---

1 Fanny Keats was born on June 3rd, 1803, and became of age the day she
received this letter. It is strange that Fanny Brawne made this error about
the date of her birthday (June 18th), but apparently she became aware of
her mistake before she wrote the next letter (the last), as she makes no
mention of the birthday and clearly regards Fanny as of age.

[June 16, 1824.]

My dear Fanny

I have this instant received your letter. I intended writing to you before thursday as I shall then go to town for two or three days, not that I had any thing particular to say for I had only mentioned the subject to my brother, who thought you had not the slightest reason to alarm yourself as Mr A. is considered beyond all dispute as a man of large property [1]—*The* losses *you mentioned are well known in the city but he is considered very rich in spite of them. As to your own affairs he thought you could at present do only what I told you, ask for an explanation, but as you have now done that I need not say any more about it, nor shall I now recommend all the* patience *and* conciliation *with Mr A. I had intended, as you seem to consider,* with me, *that he has acted to the best of his* judgement. *You are now at liberty and may do as you like and I hope one of the first things you do will be to come and see me, you must fix your own time and I leave it to you because you will know what to do so as not to offend*

*Mr or Mrs Abbey who having been used so long to have
their own way, may like you to act for yourself with as
much* civility *to them as you can make it convenient to
show.—I shall return home on Saturday and I have no en-
gagement till after the first two or three days in July, then
I expect to go to Hampton but the time is not yet fixed nor
can I exactly tell when I can go, as I have been invited to
go to Cambridge in July and I must know the time for
that expedition before I can determine on the other. If
you well can come and see me now, do, I am very impatient
to see you but do not like to press you too much least I should
persuade you to do what you do not think right, this much
I must say that nothing would give me so much pleasure.
I cannot send this note till I can see my cousins to enquire
whether there is any more particular name for the quadrilles
than I am acquainted with. This letter has been kept back
a whole day because, though I wrote immediately to my
cousin to know the set of quadrilles and she came here pur-
posely to tell me we each forgot to mention the subject.*

'Musard's 17th *Set from the* Gazza Ladra' [2] *is the one
I like, and after that Hart's* 7th *Set from Pietro L'Eremite
but it is not necessary to do more that* [for *than*] *to mention*

the numbers of the set, I give you the name of the Opera
to make you more certain

I remain my dear Fanny

Yours very sincerely

F B—

Finished wednesday night.

POSTMARK: Fenchurch St. 17 June. 1824.
ADDRESS: *For Miss Keats*
at Richard Abbey's Esq.
Marsh Street
Walthamstow.

1 After she became of age Fanny Keats had considerable difficulty in obtaining from Richard Abbey the money of which he had control. Charles Wentworth Dilke came to her aid, and eventually she received not only her share of the money left by her grandmother, but also that due to her from the estates of her brothers John and Tom.

2 *La Gazza Ladra* ('The Thieving Magpie'), comic opera, music by Rossini, first produced in London on Mar. 10th, 1821. *Pietro l'Eremita* (better known as *Mosè in Egitto*), opera, music by Rossini, first produced in London on Apr. 23rd, 1822.

INDEX

Reference to the notes are indicated by the use of italic figures